Trace Letters
Learn to write letters and numbers, sight words and sentences

This book belongs to:

____

This book will help your child take their first steps towards the fun world of letters.
This workbook is gradually structured in a way that builds your child's confidence and ability to write.

Part 1: Line tracing & Writing letters
Part 2: Writing sight words
Part 3:Writing simple sentences
Part 4: Writing numbers (0-100)

To encourage writing development, guidance from a parent, caregiver, or teacher is necessary.

Hello!
I am Isabela and my passion is introducing kids to the wonderful world of letters and numbers.
I want you to experience how fun writing can be! This is why I have created this Handwriting Practice Workbook.
So, if you liked this book encourage your parents to leave a review.
Your thoughts and opinions are very important to me.
This is how I keep creating workbooks like this!
Also, as a bonus, when your book is completed you can claim a free certificate by following the instructions at the end of the workbook.
Thank you!

Hi!
I am buzzy. I want to be your friend and guide you through the journey of learning.
We'll have so much fun together!

About Writing

Handwriting is an essential life skill that helps children develop reading and spelling skills.

3 Steps to Writing

- Tracing
- Learning to write the alphabet and numbers
- Learning to write words and sentences

- Handwriting is a complex skill that develops over time.
- To learn handwriting children need to combine fine motor skills, language, memory, and concentration.
- They also need to practice and follow instructions.

Tracing is beneficial because it helps build:

- Fine motor skill
- Pre-writing skills
- Concentration and focus
- Visual-spatial skills
- Creativity and drawing skills

PART 1

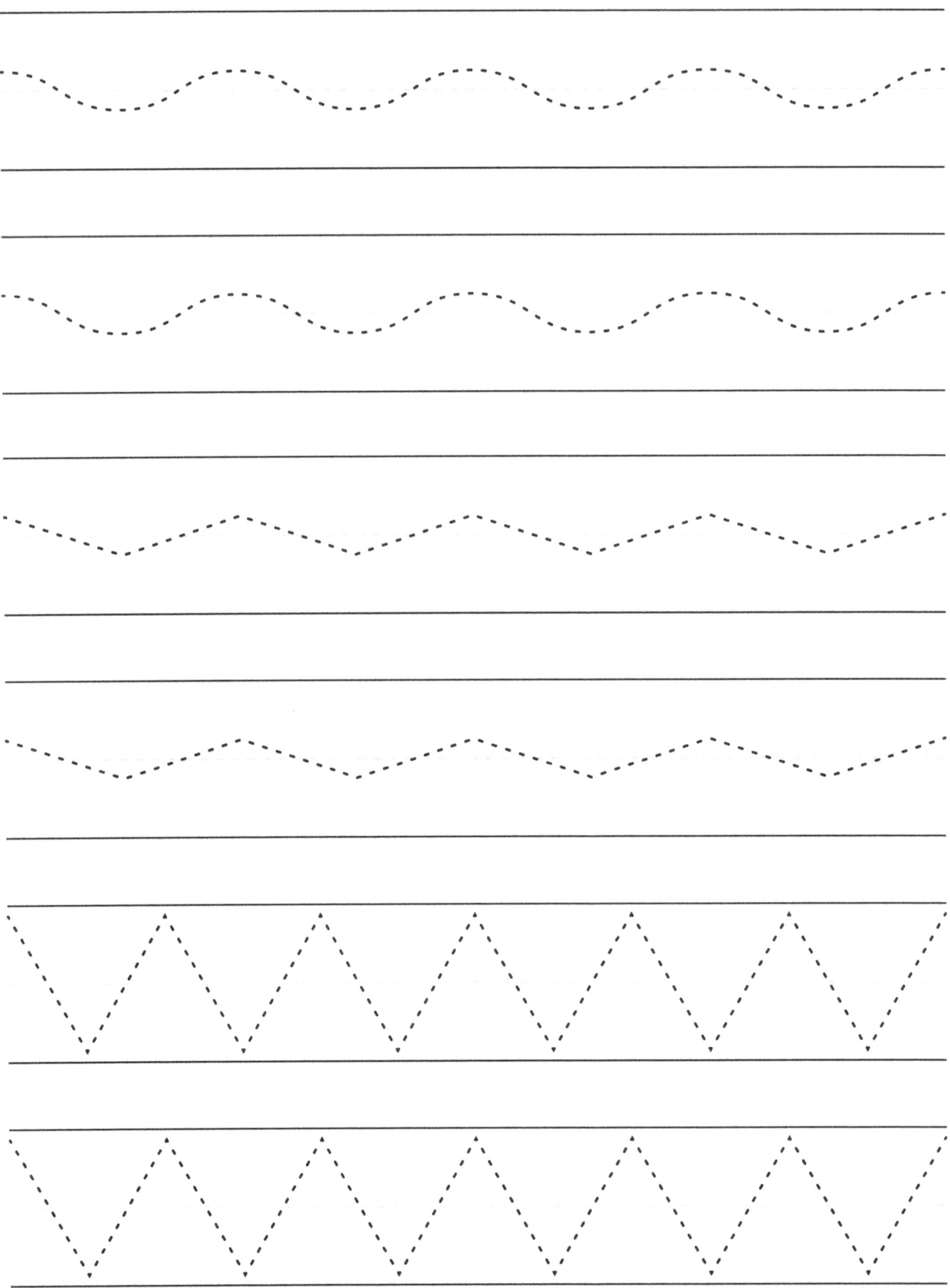

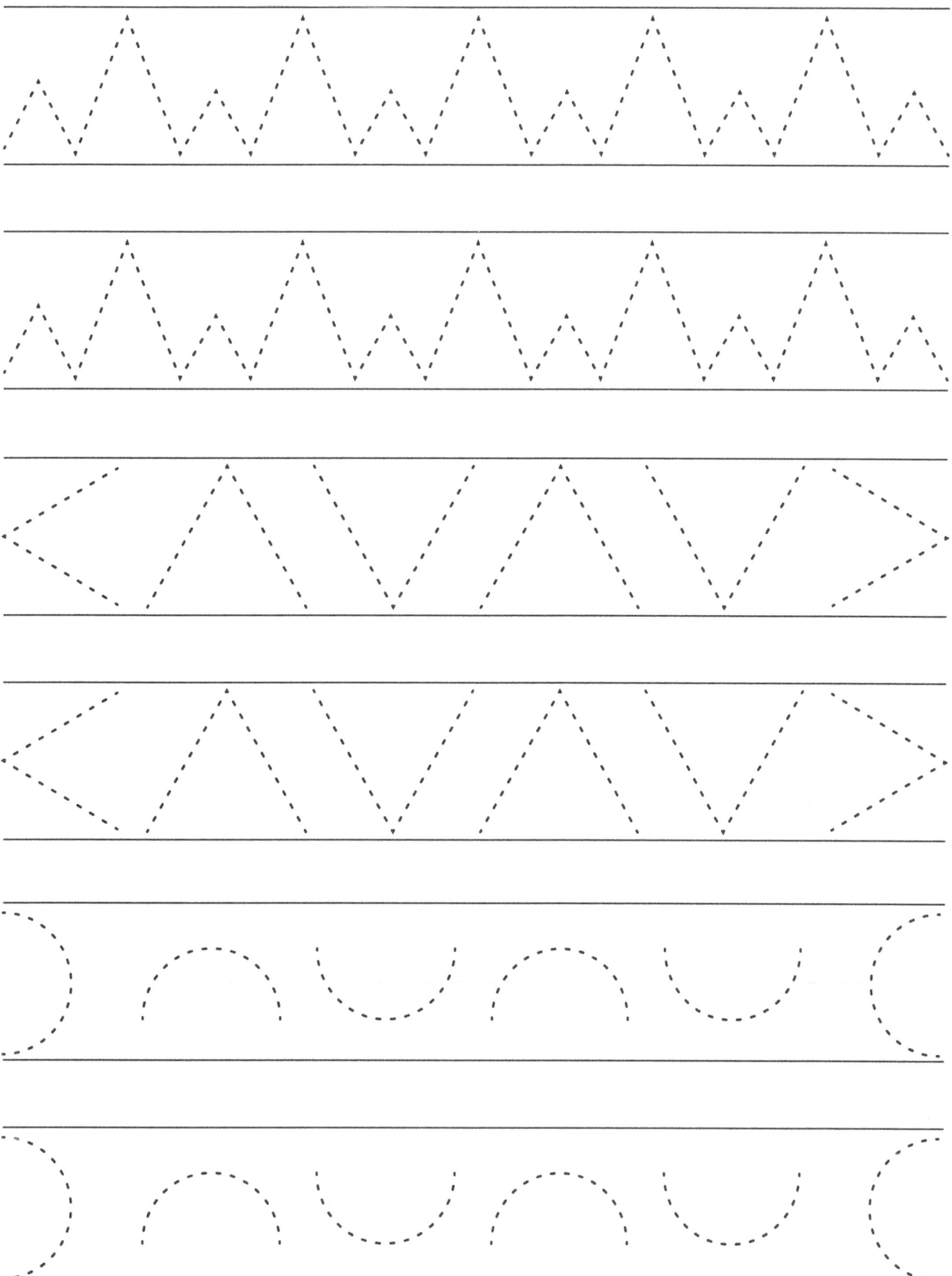

Name: _______   Date: _______

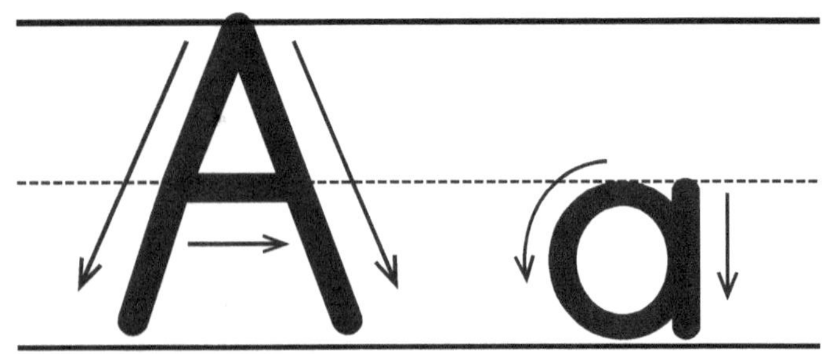

Apple

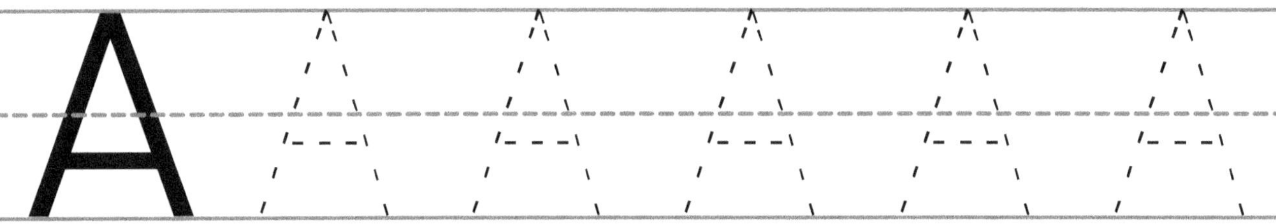

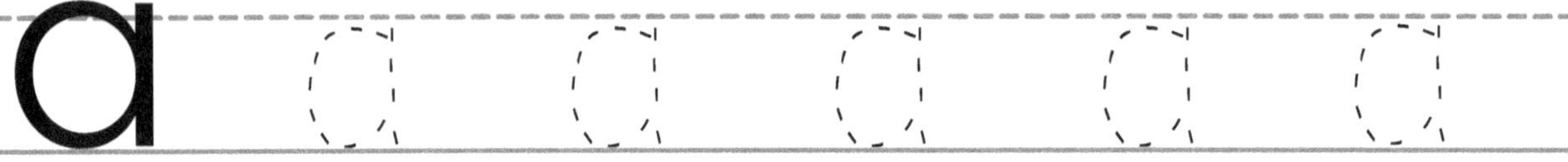

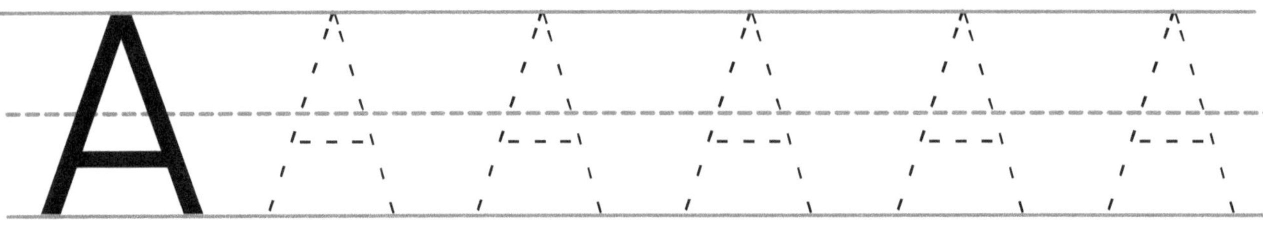

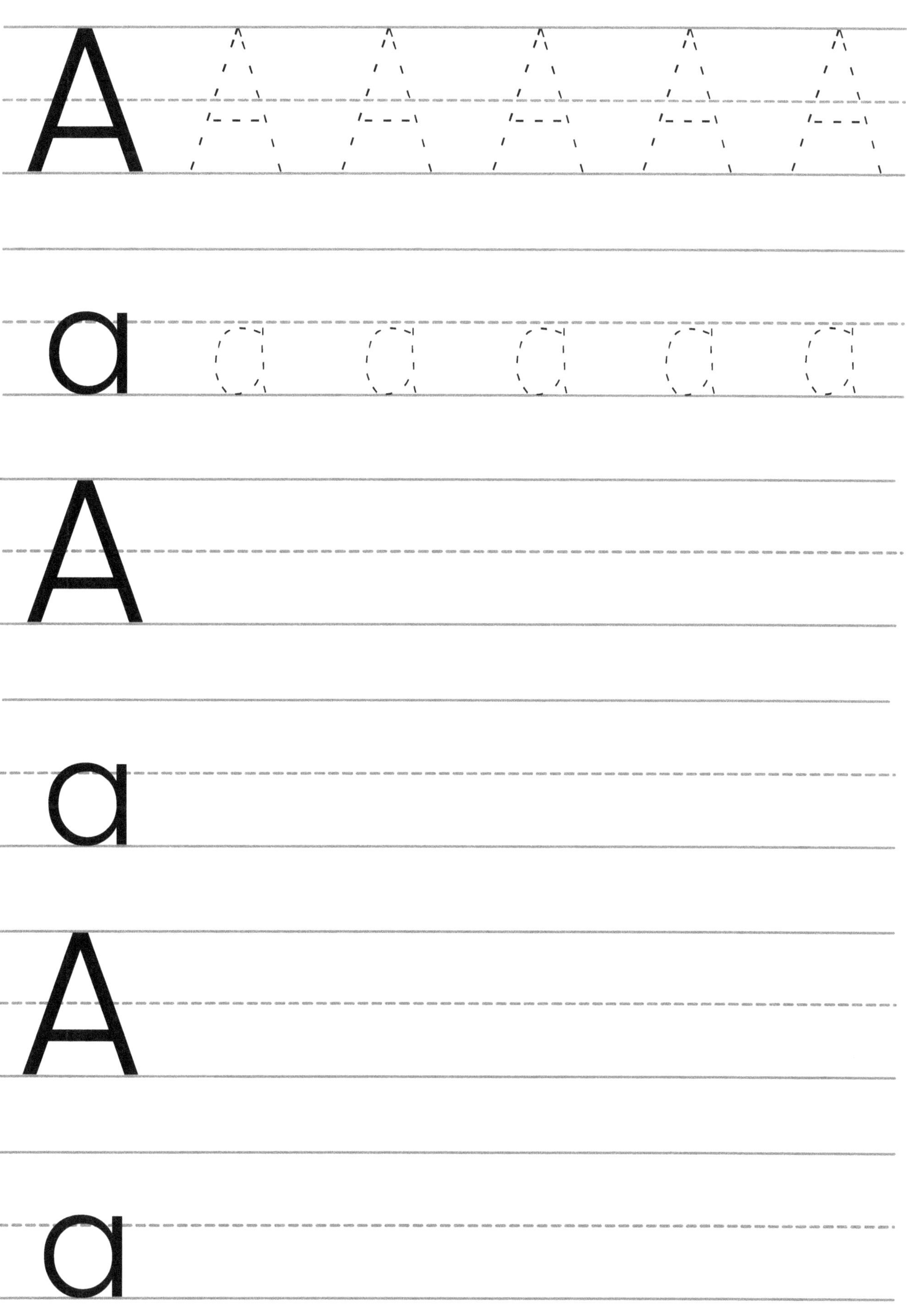

Trace the letters and then practice writing them on your own!

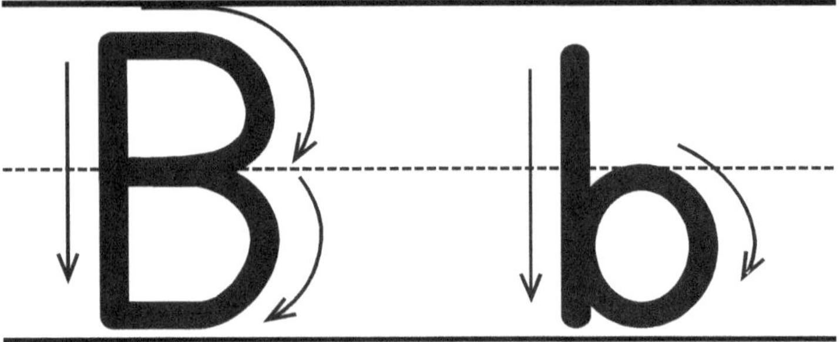

Butterfly

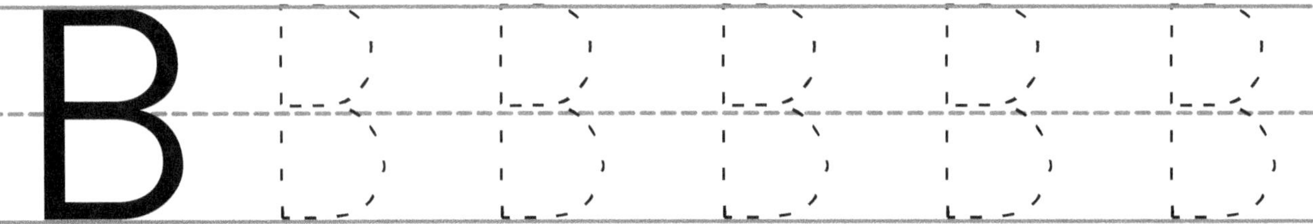

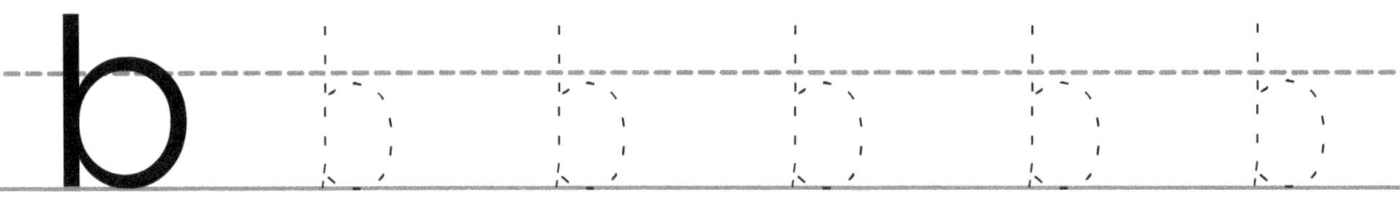

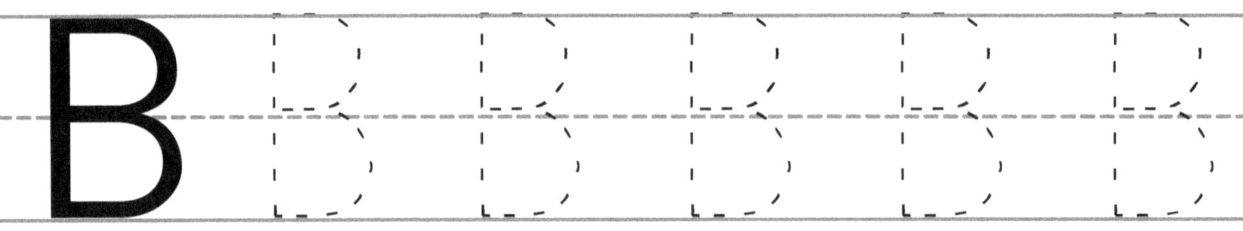

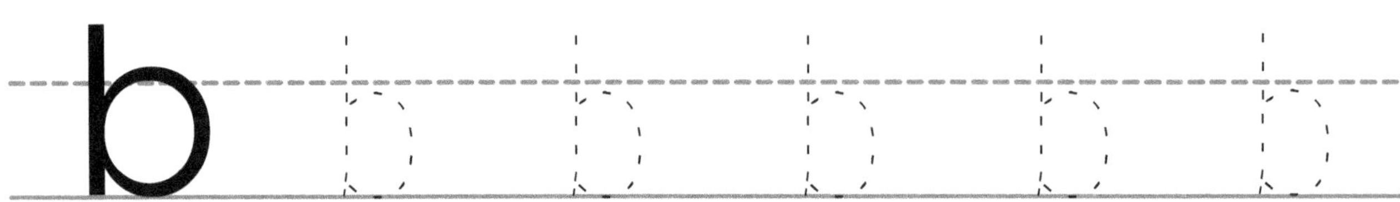

B b b b b b b B

b b b b b b

B

b

B

b

Trace the letters and then practice writing them on your own!

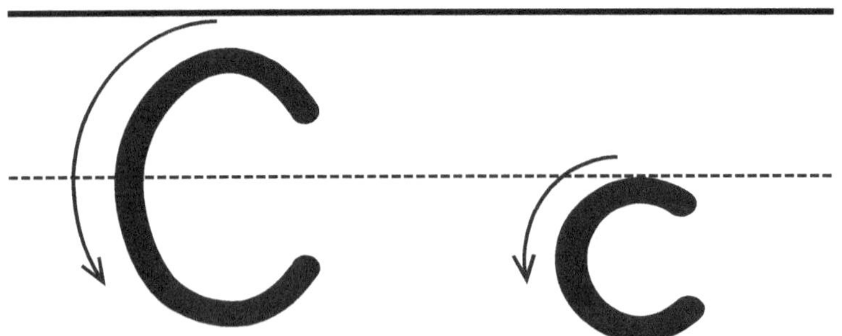

Cat

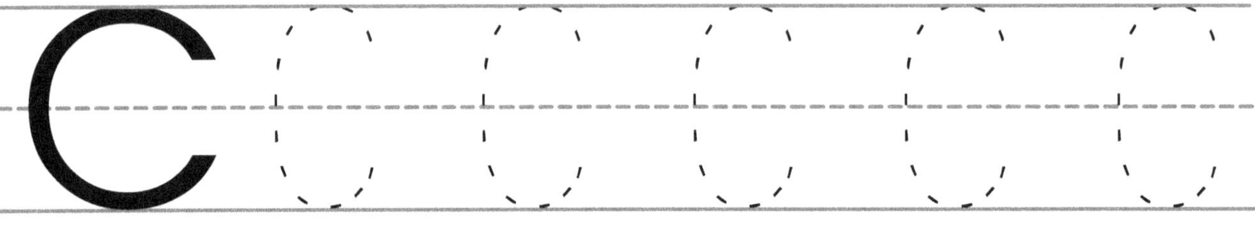

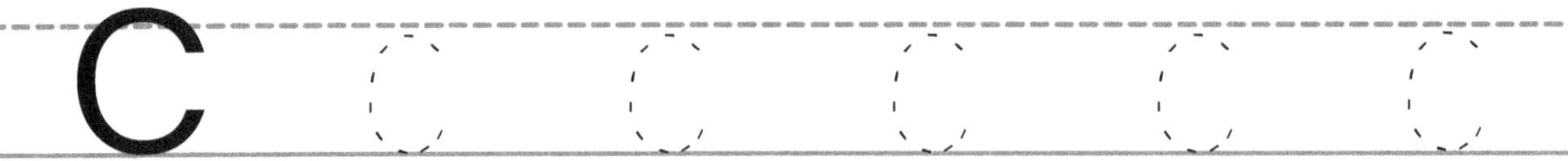

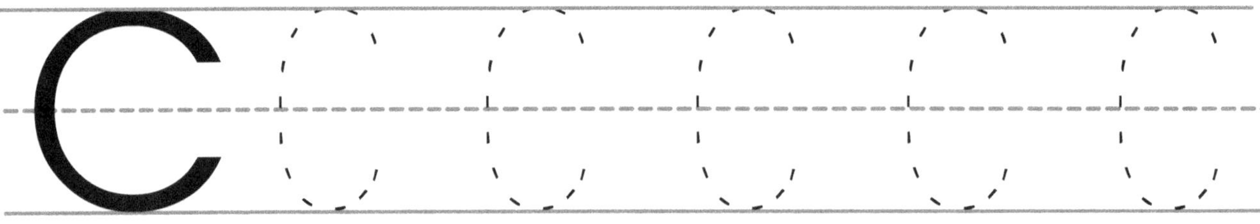

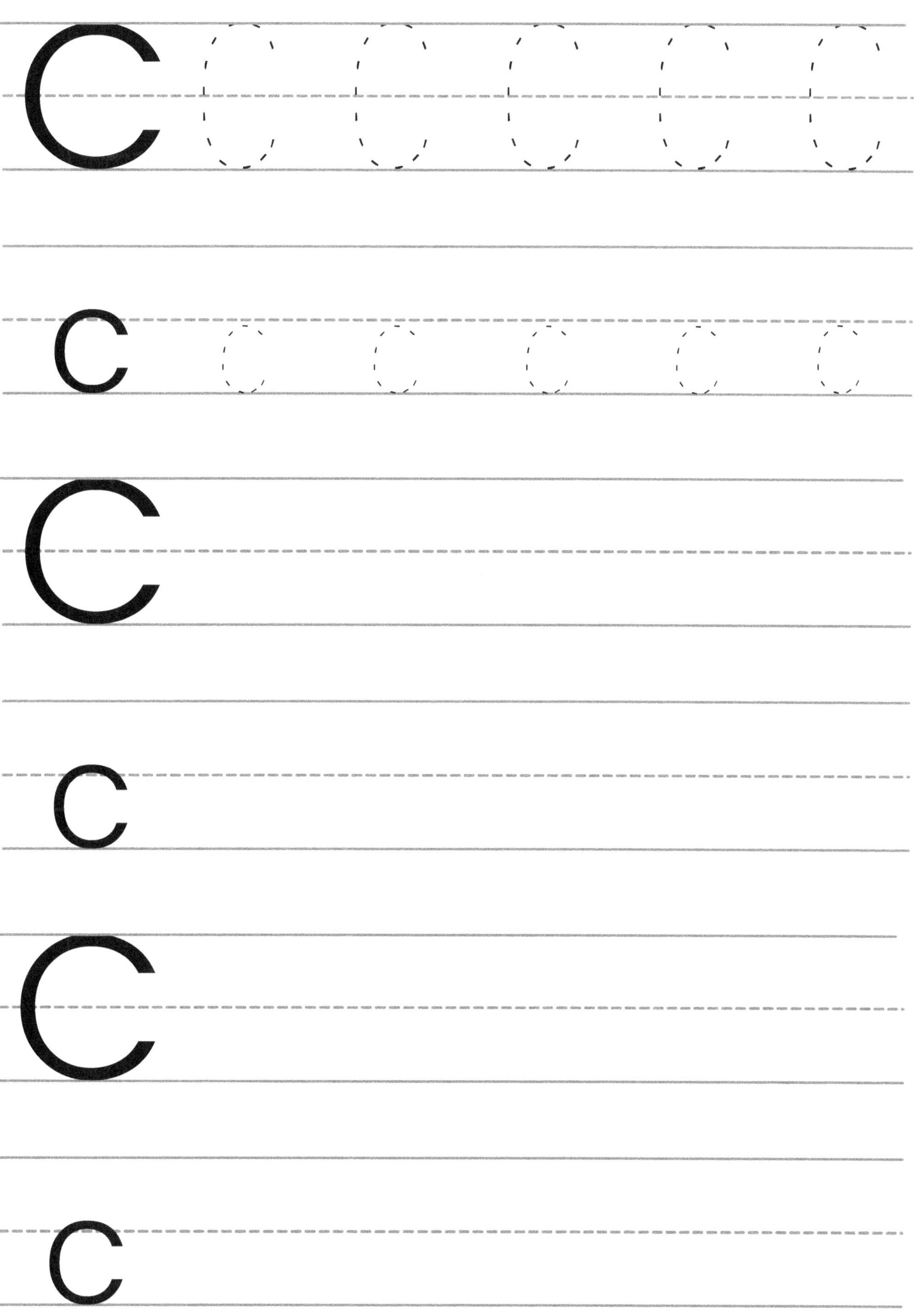

Trace the letters and then practice writing them on your own!

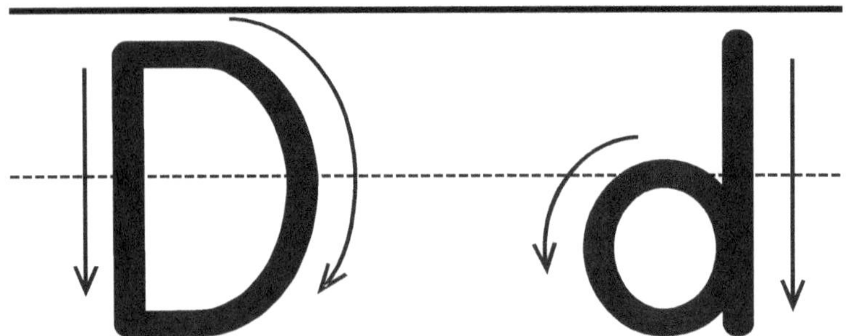

Dinosaur

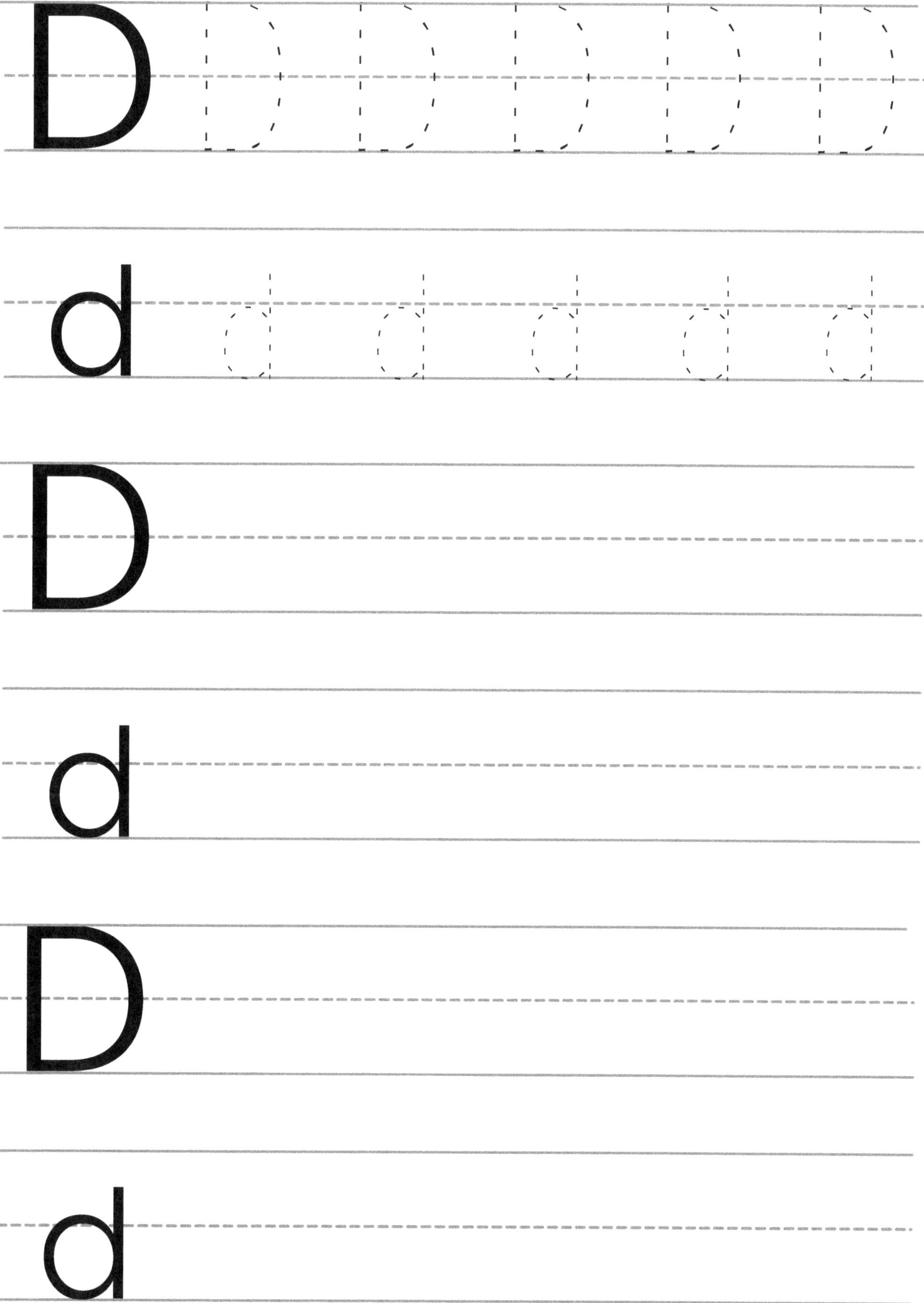

Trace the letters and then practice writing them on your own!

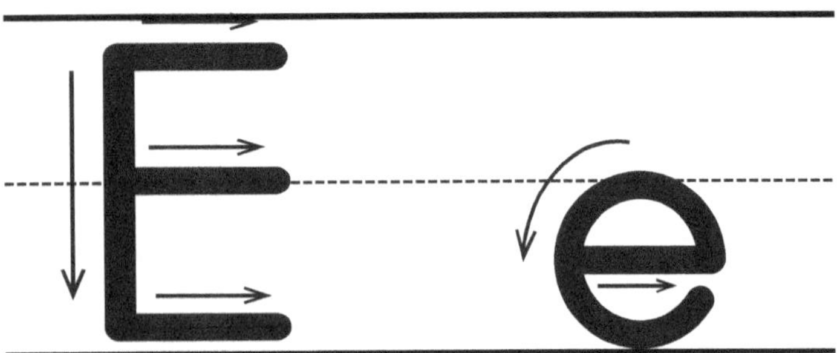

Elephant

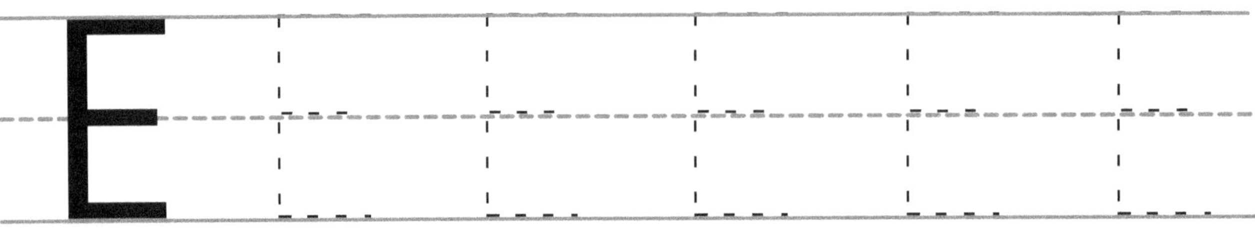

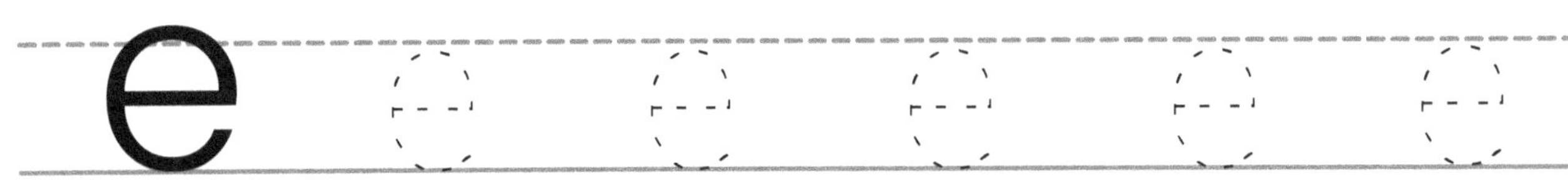

Trace the letters and then practice writing them on your own!

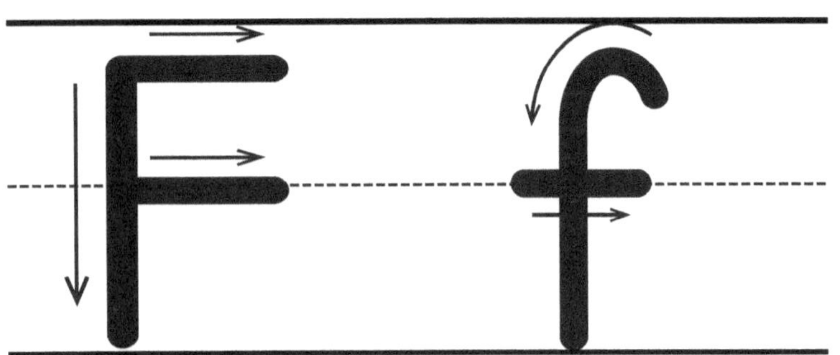

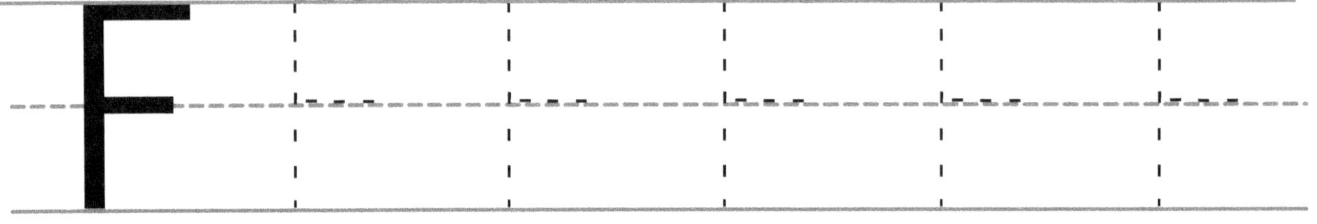

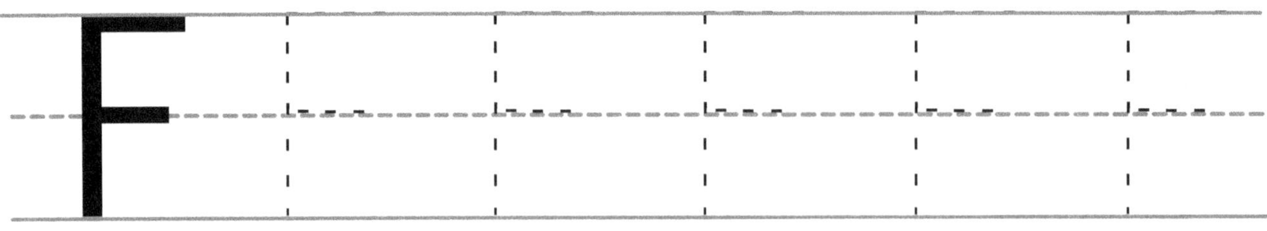

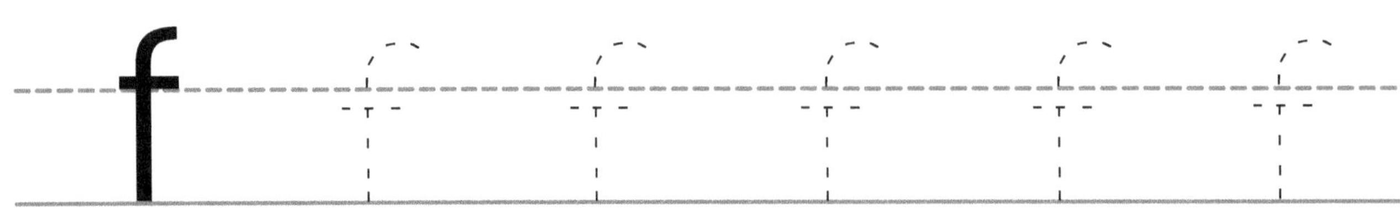

Trace the letters and then practice writing them on your own!

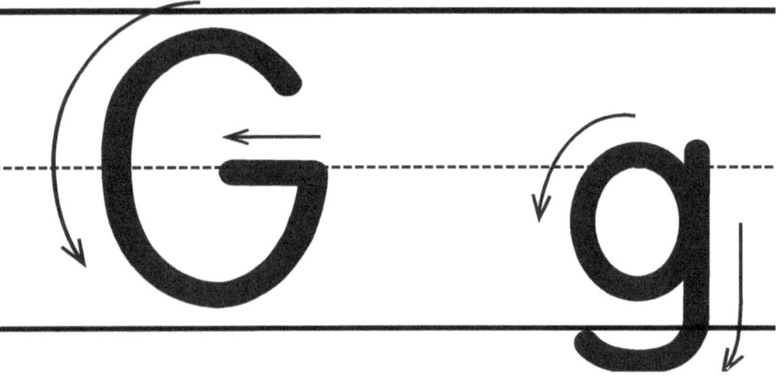

Giraffe

G G G G G G

g g g g g g

G G G G G G

g g g g g g

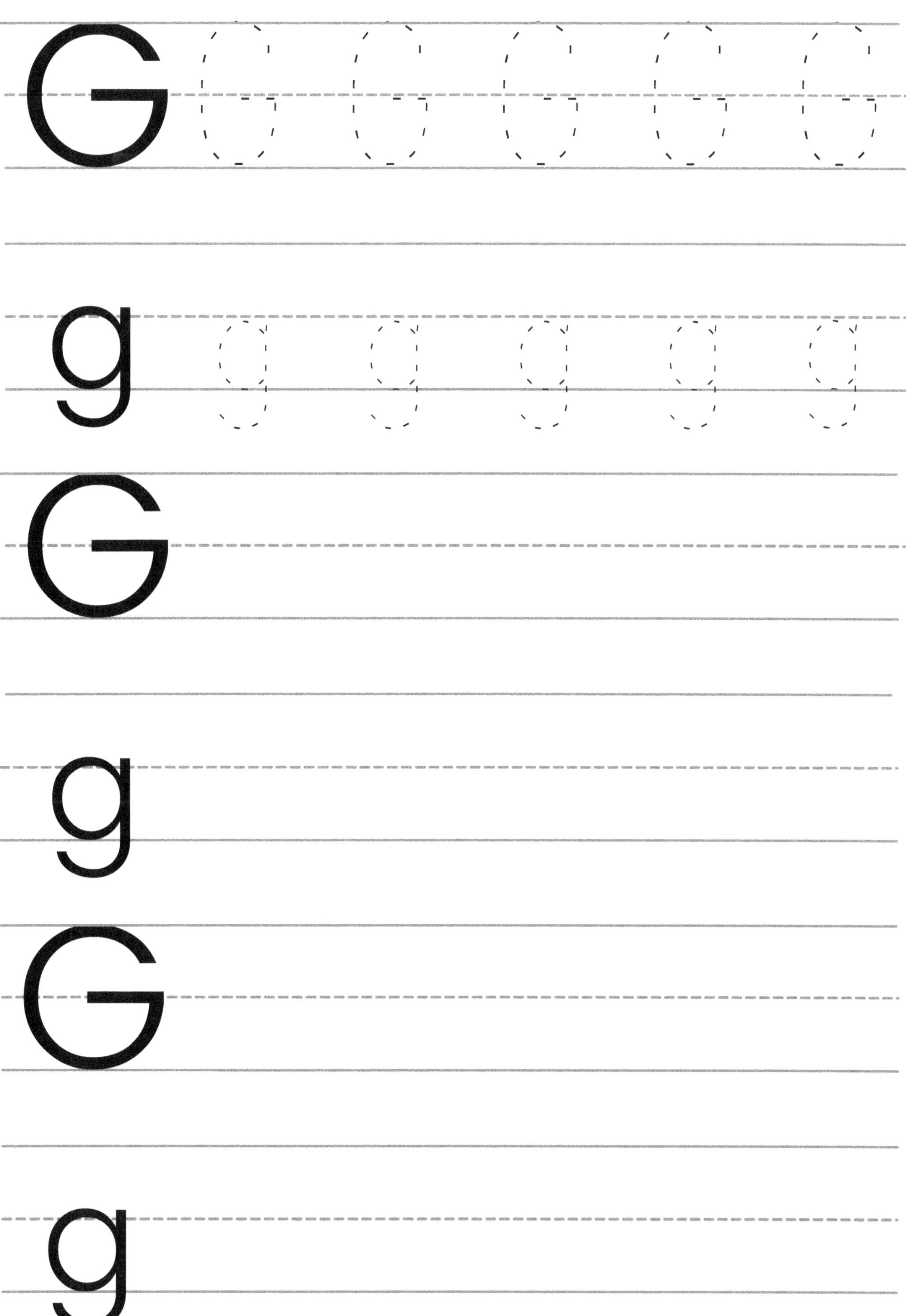

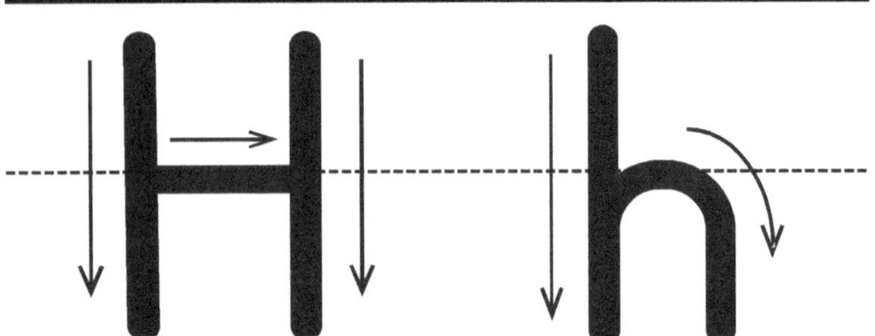

Trace the letters and then practice
writing them on your own!

Horse

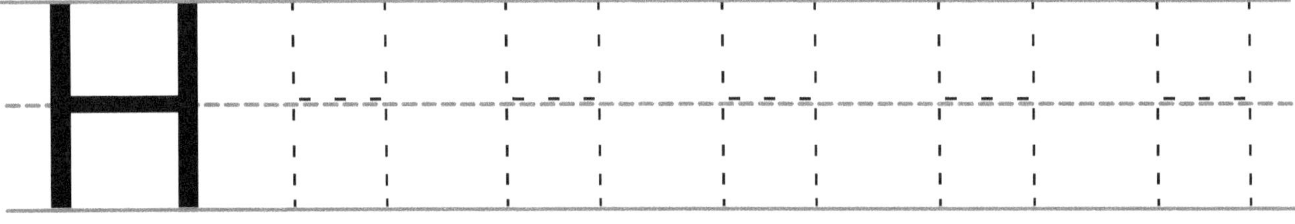

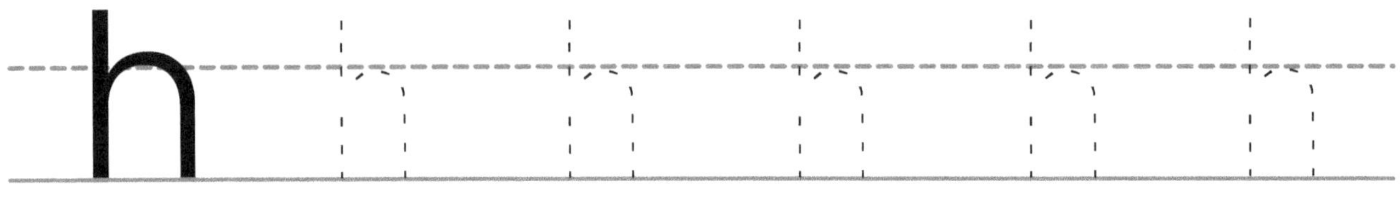

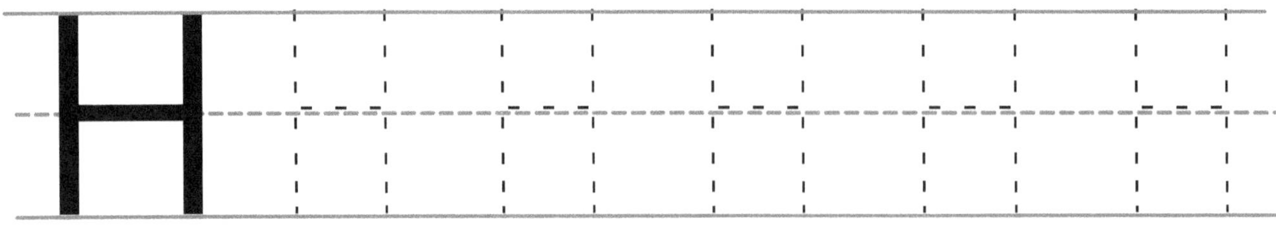

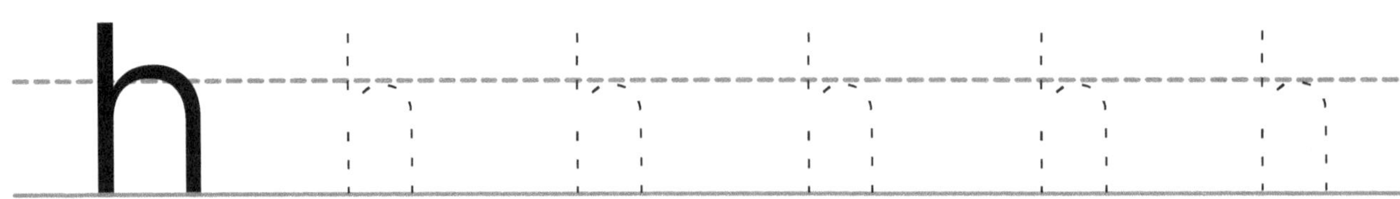

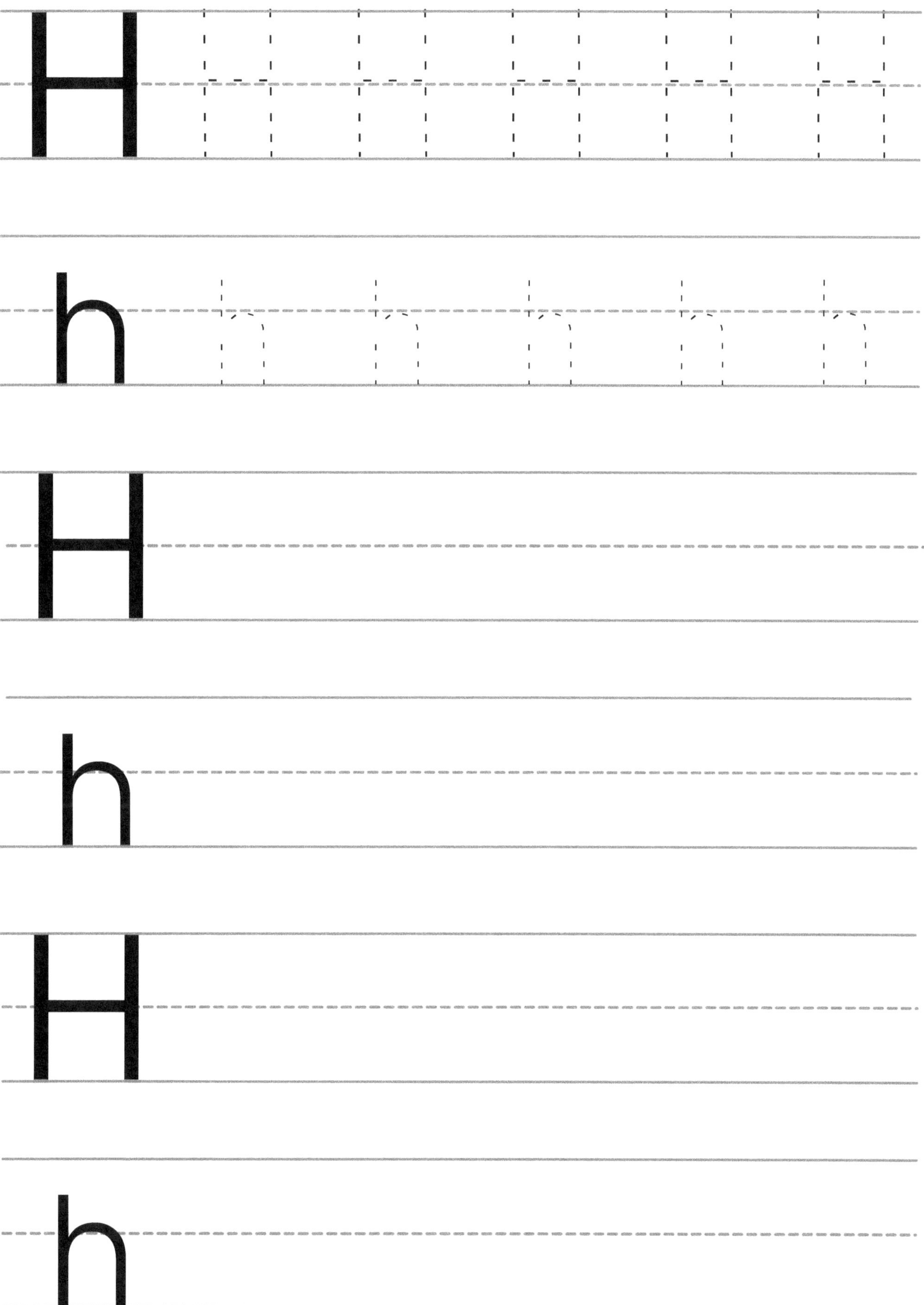

Name: _______________ Date: _______________

Trace the letters and then practice writing them on your own!

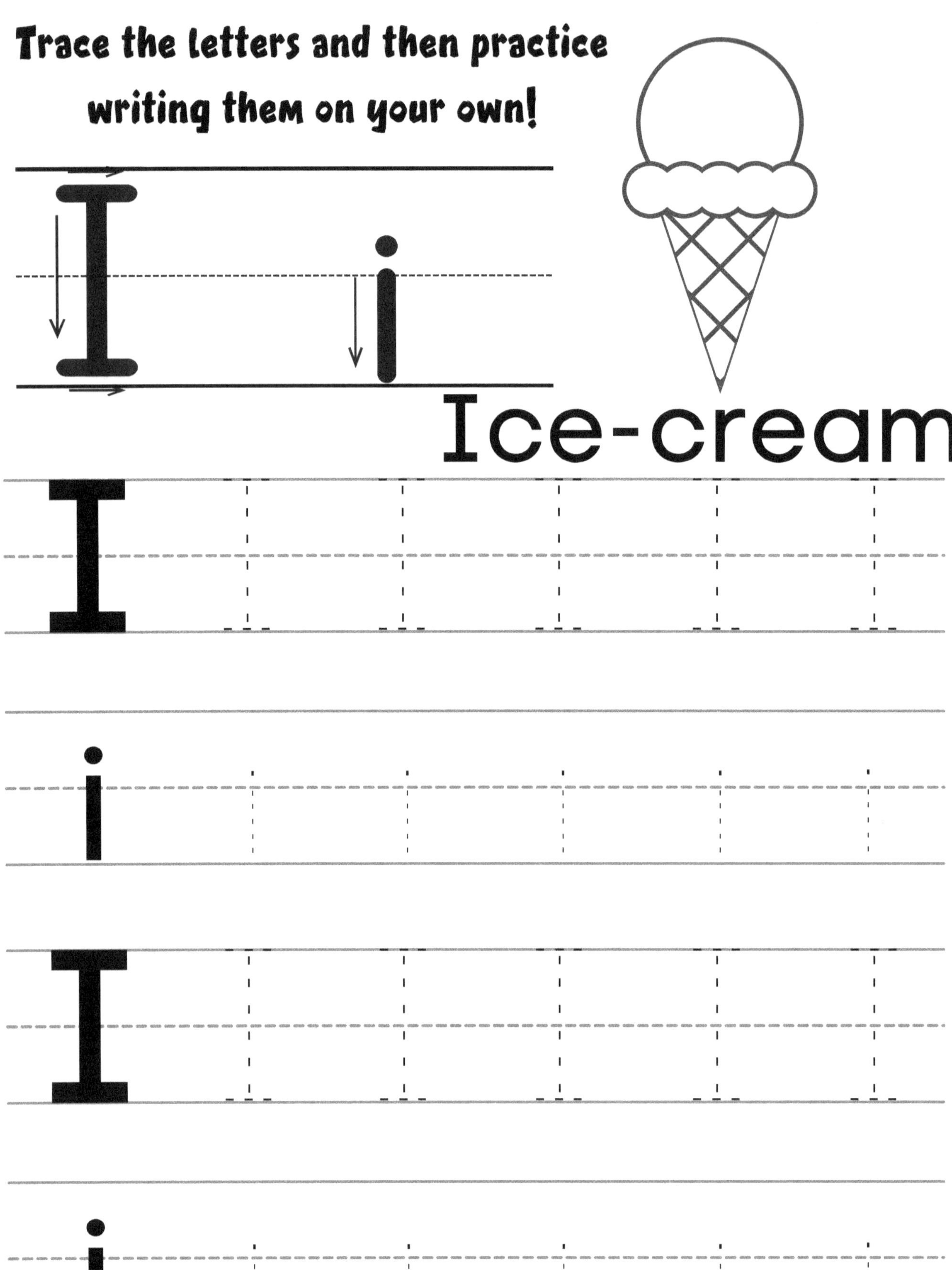

Ice-cream

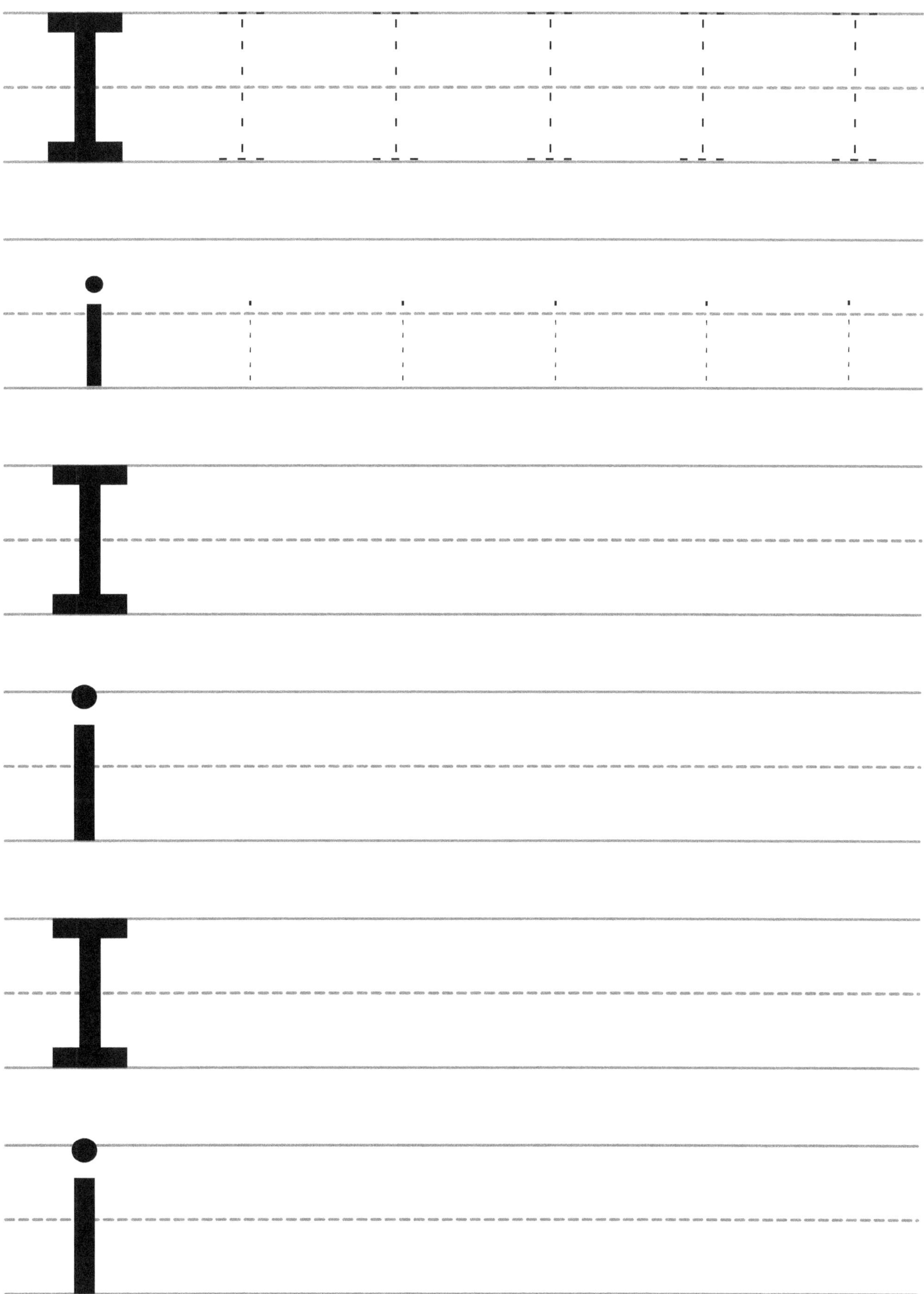

Trace the letters and then practice writing them on your own!

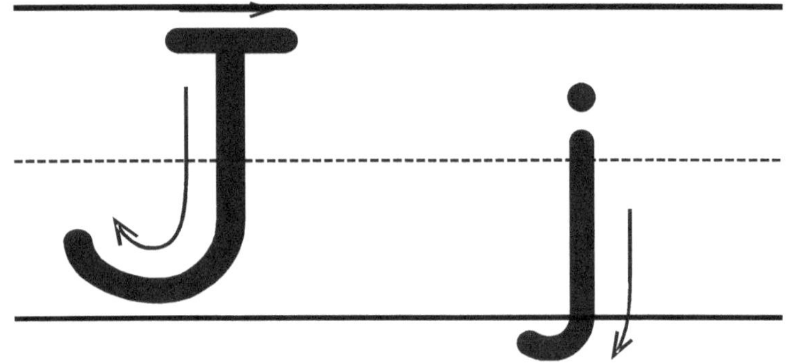

Jam

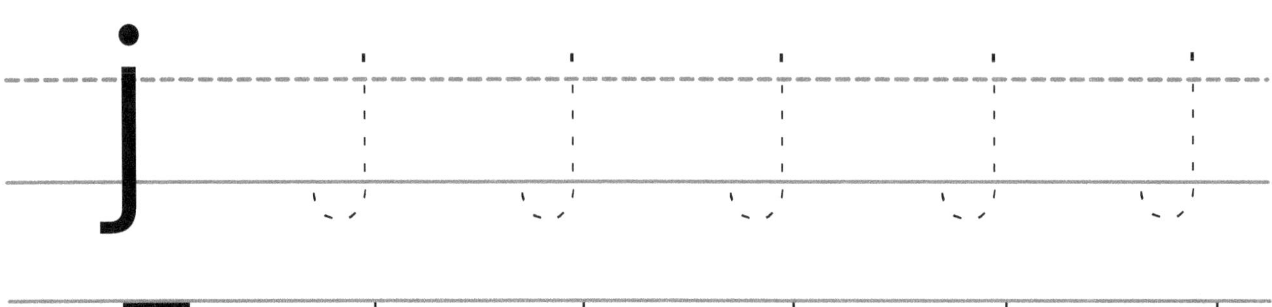

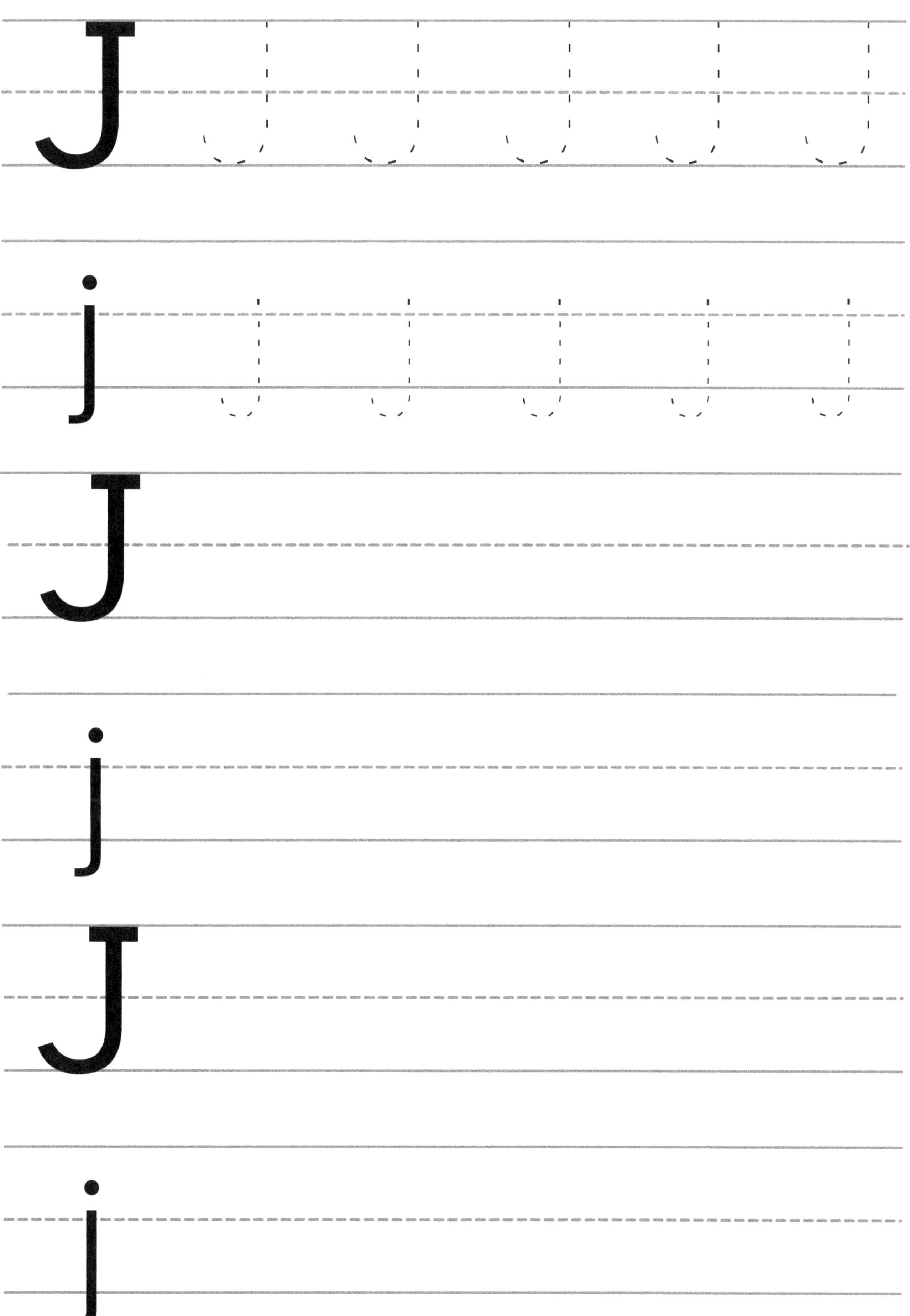

Trace the letters and then practice writing them on your own!

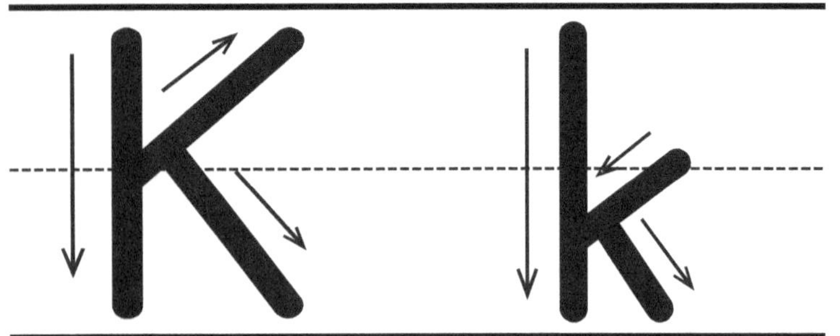

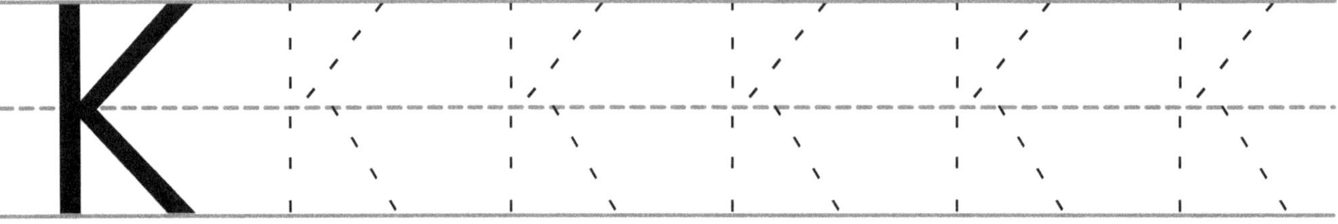

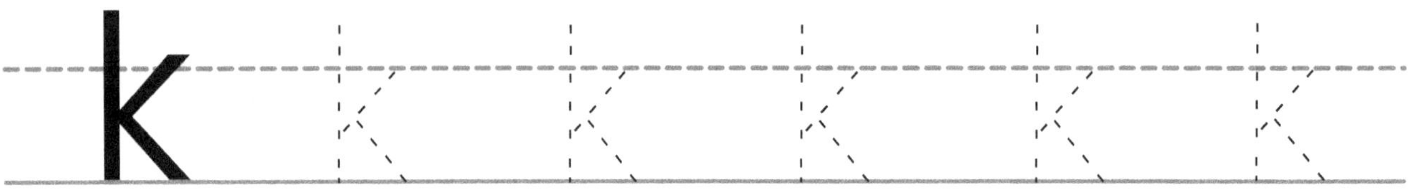

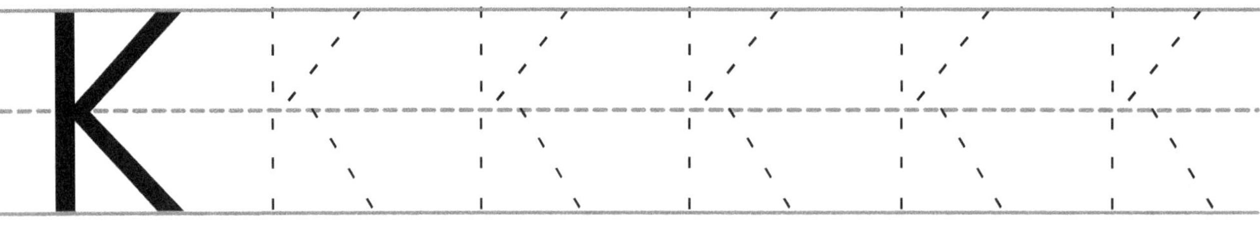

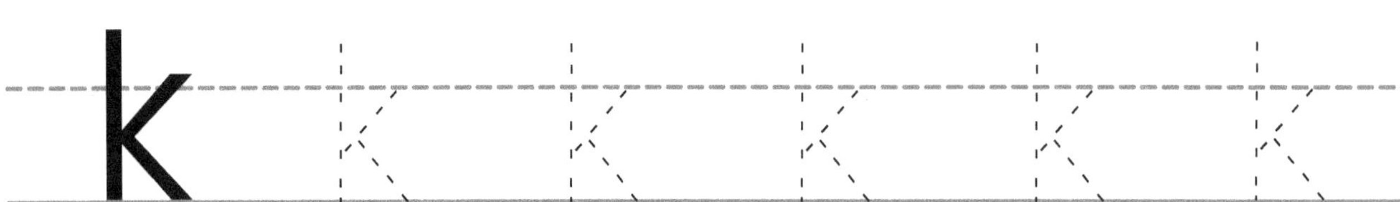

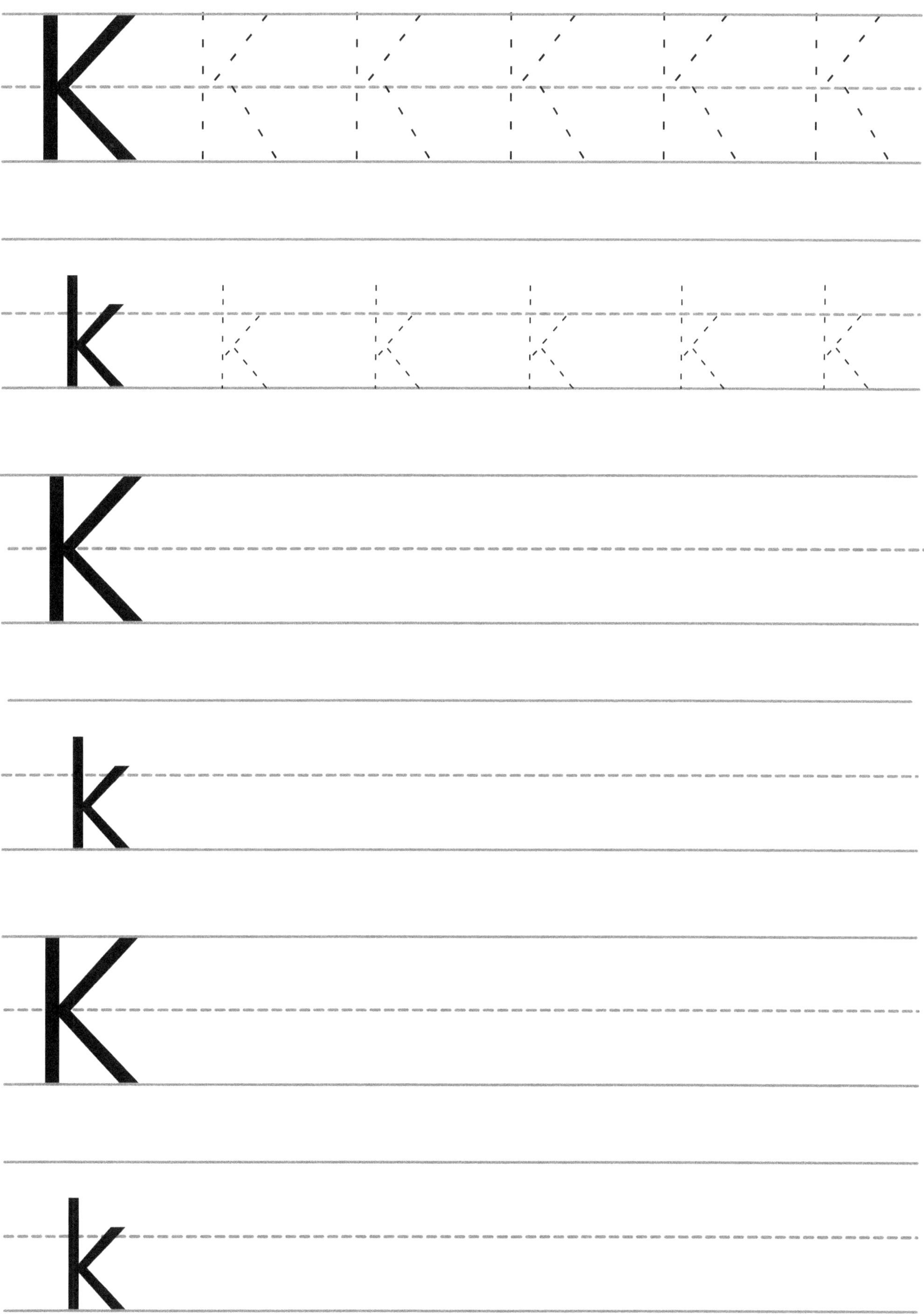

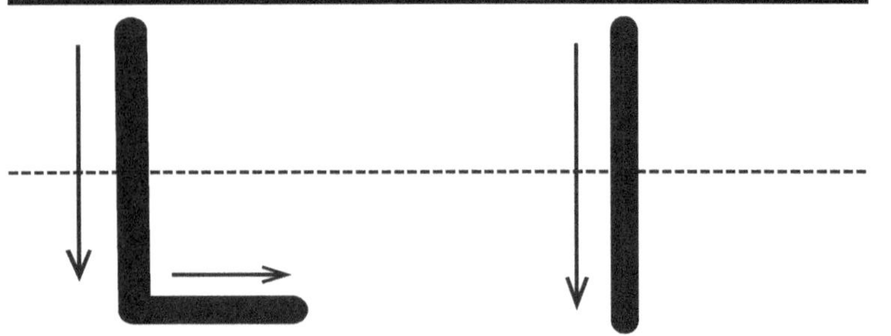

Trace the letters and then practice
writing them on your own!

Lion

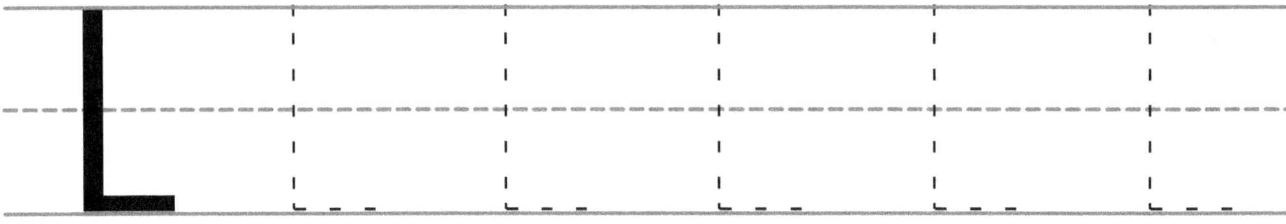

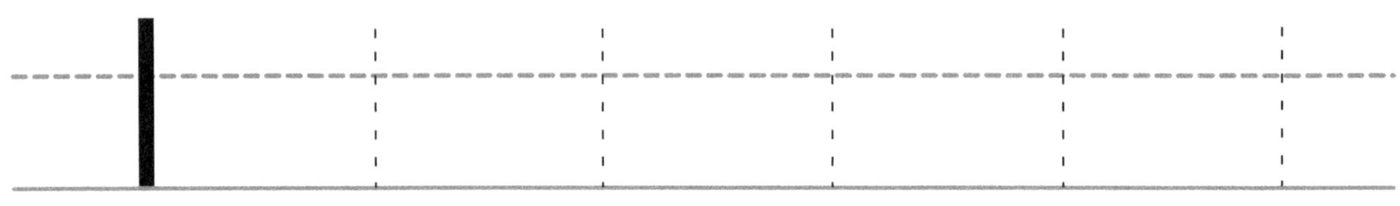

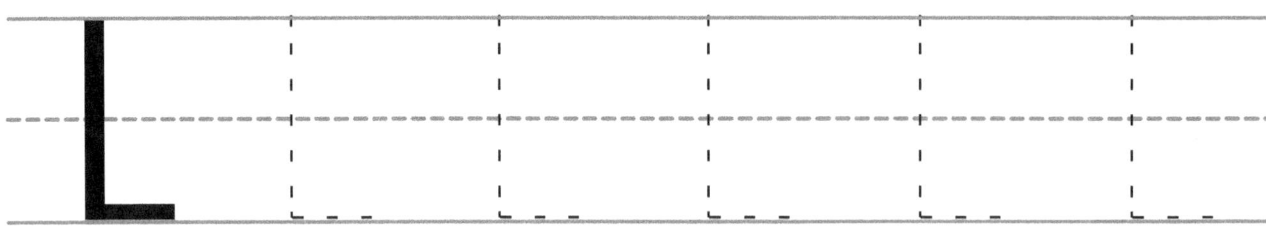

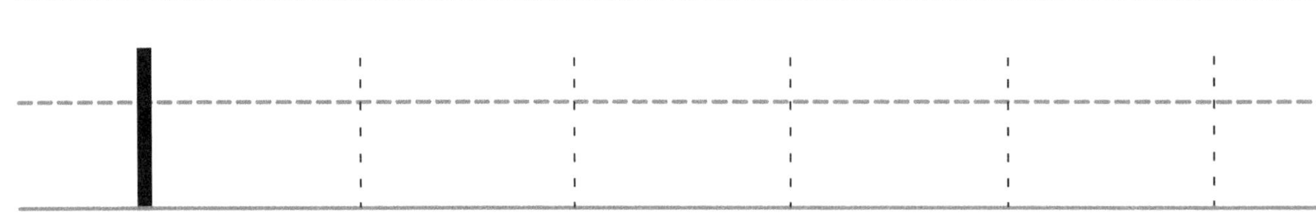

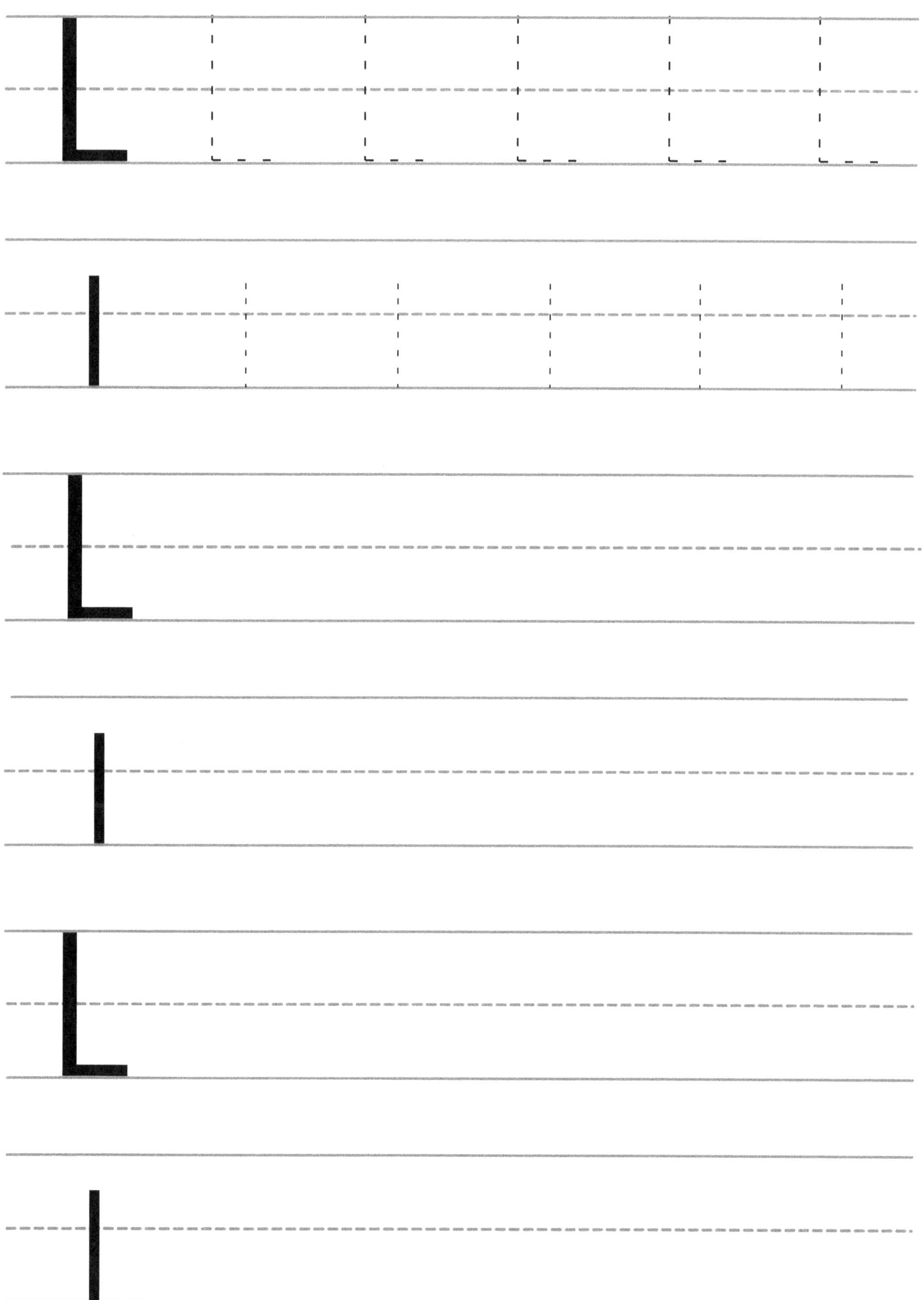

Trace the letters and then practice writing them on your own!

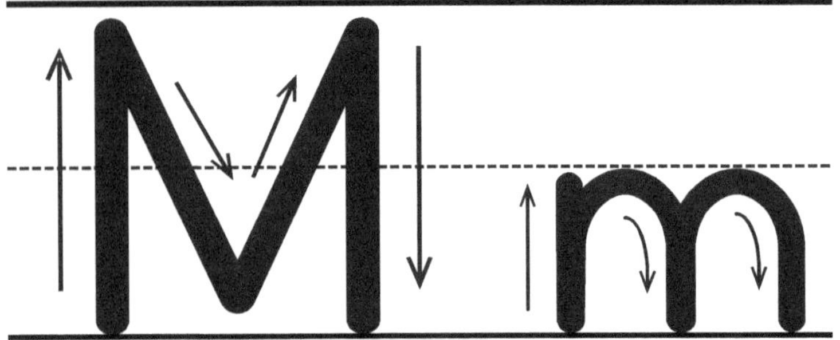

Monkey

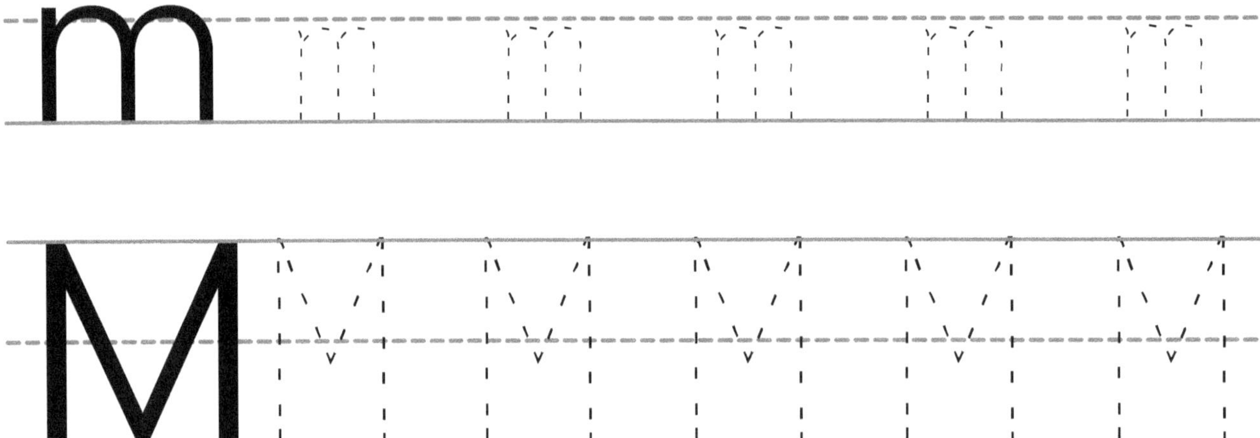

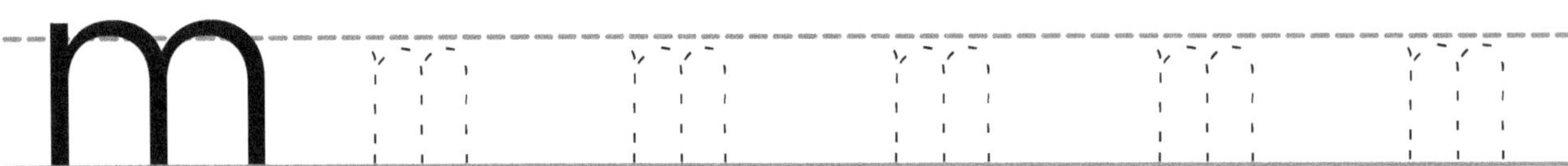

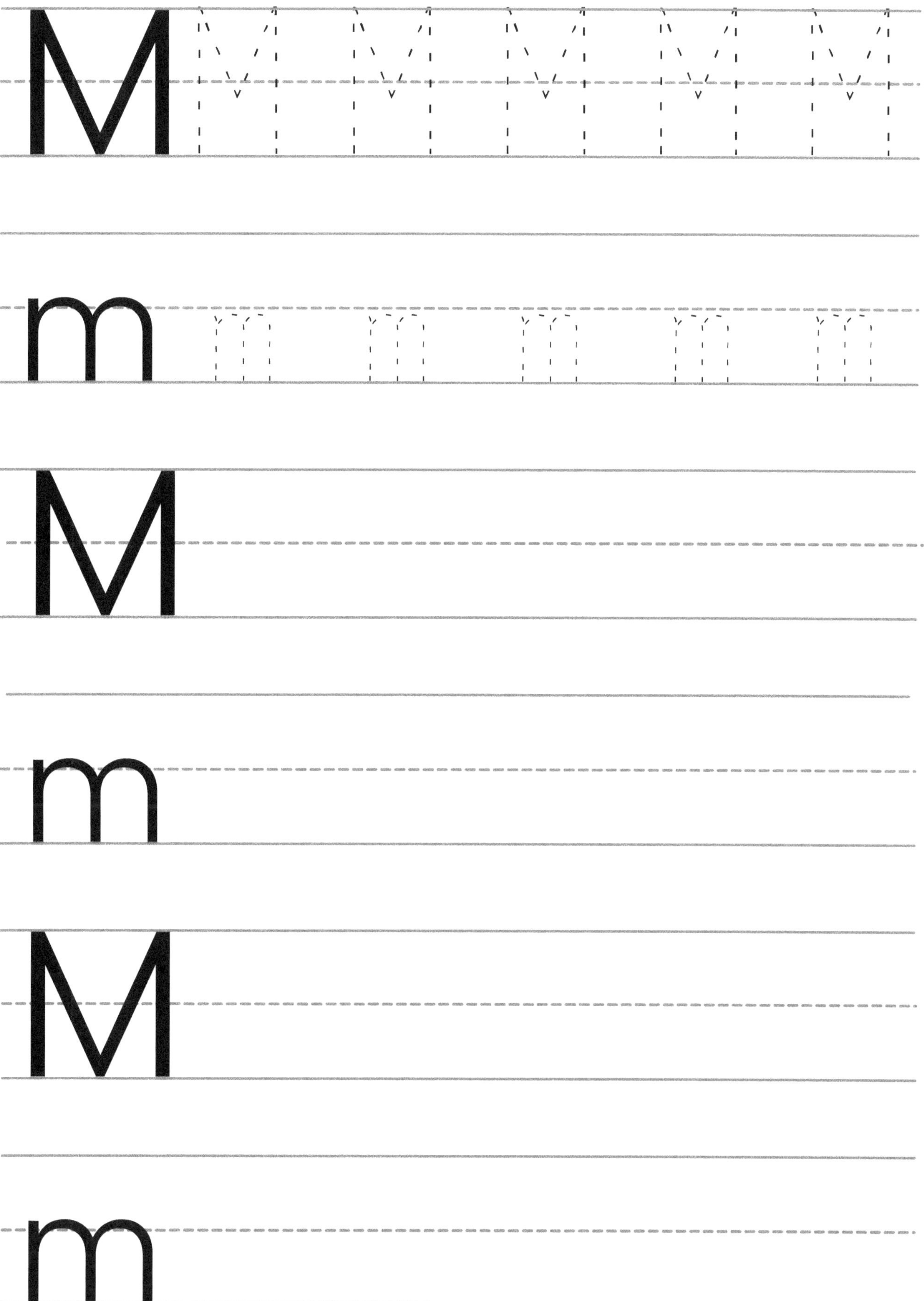

Trace the letters and then practice writing them on your own!

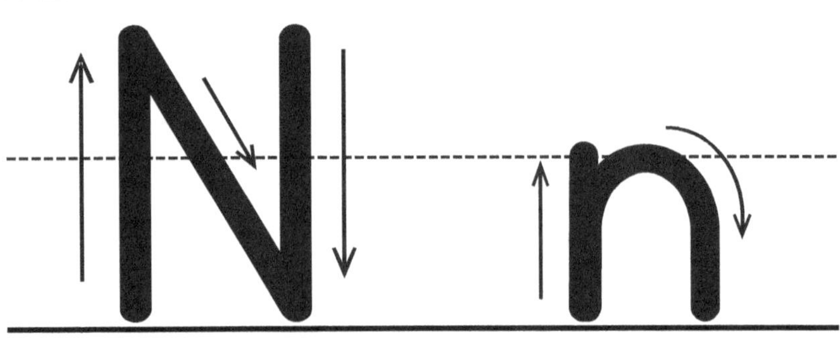

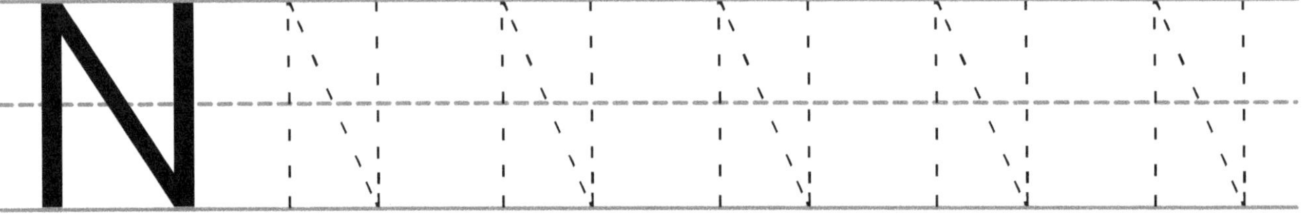

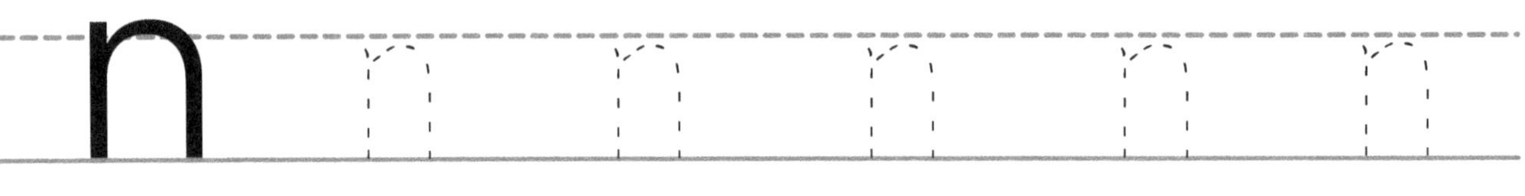

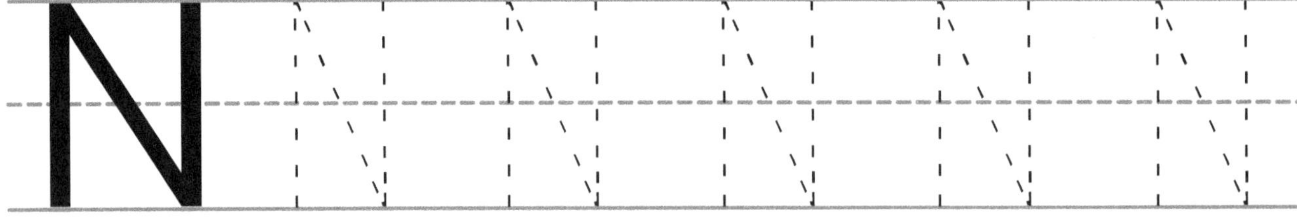

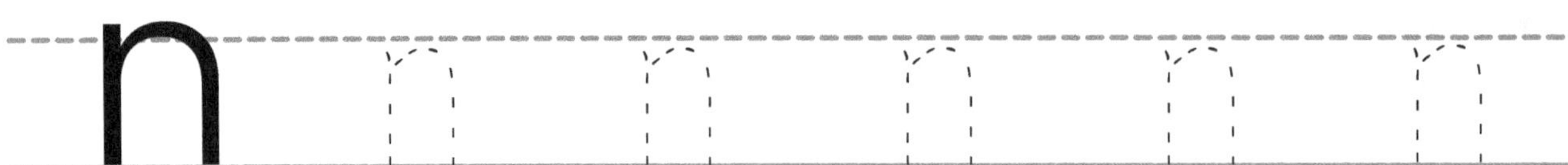

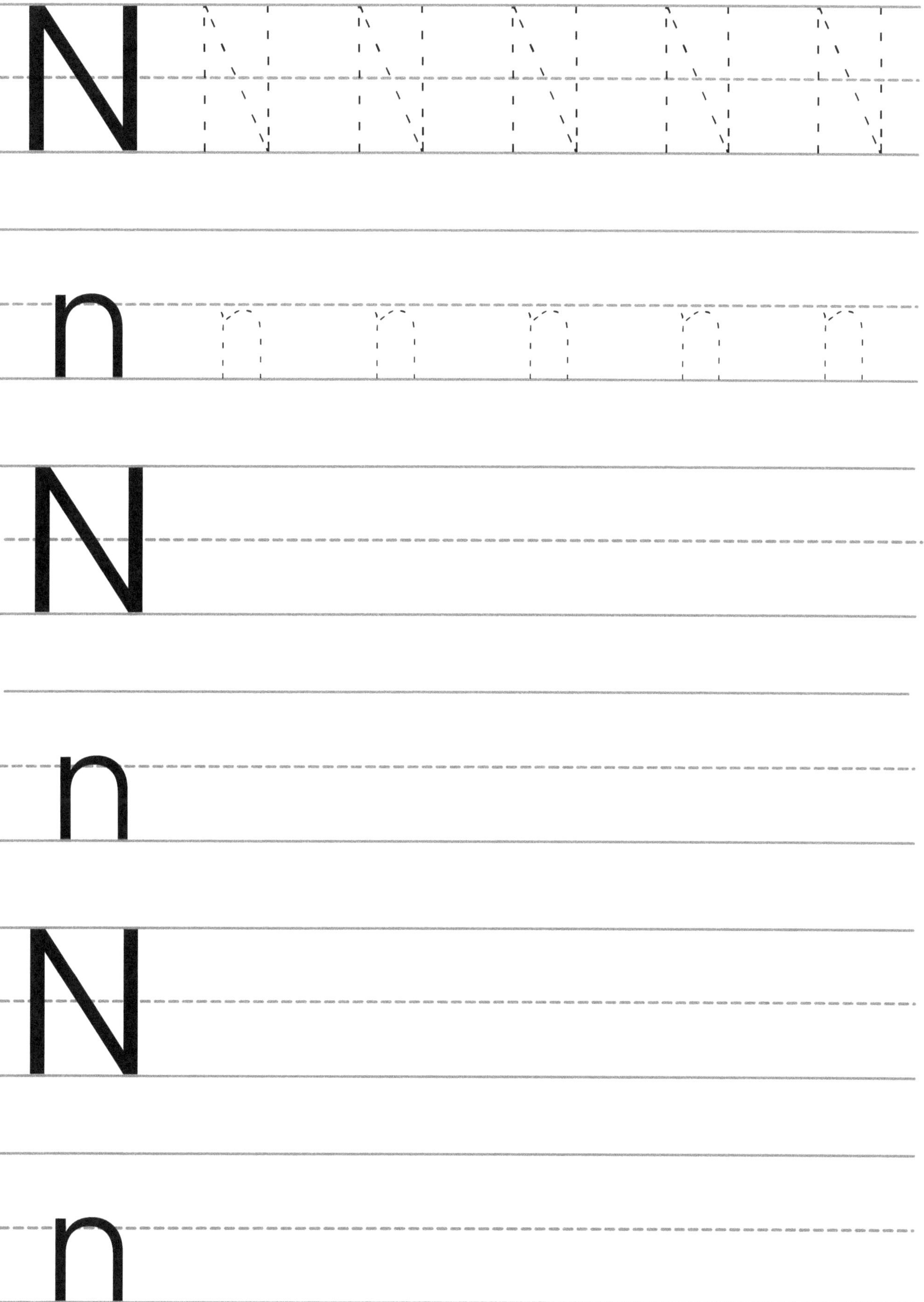

Trace the letters and then practice writing them on your own!

O O O O O O

O O O O O O

O

O O O O O O

O

O O O O O O

Name: _______________ Date: _______________

Trace the letters and then practice writing them on your own!

P p

Penguin

P

p

P

p

P

p

P

p

P

p

Trace the letters and then practice writing them on your own!

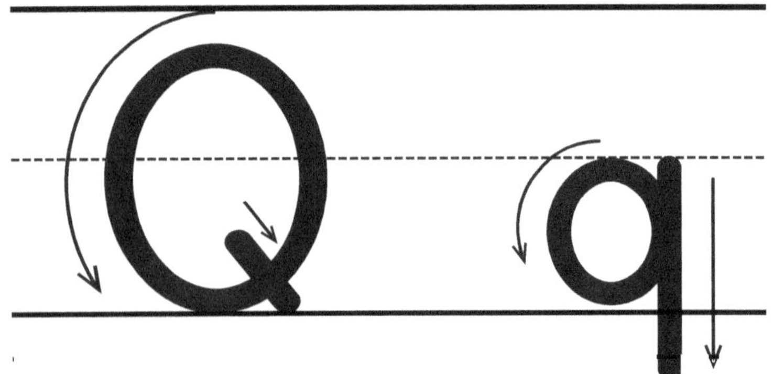

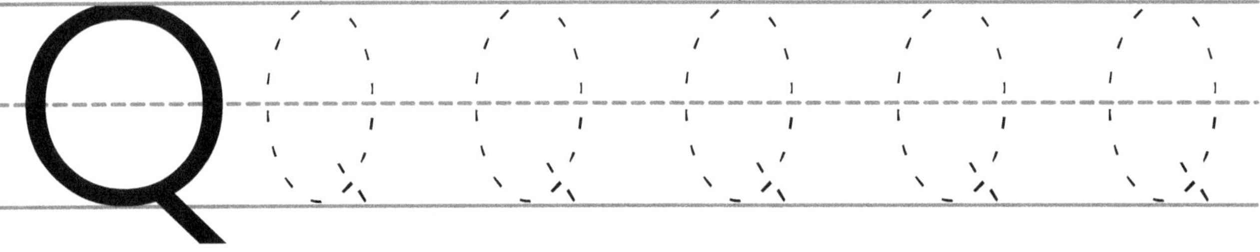

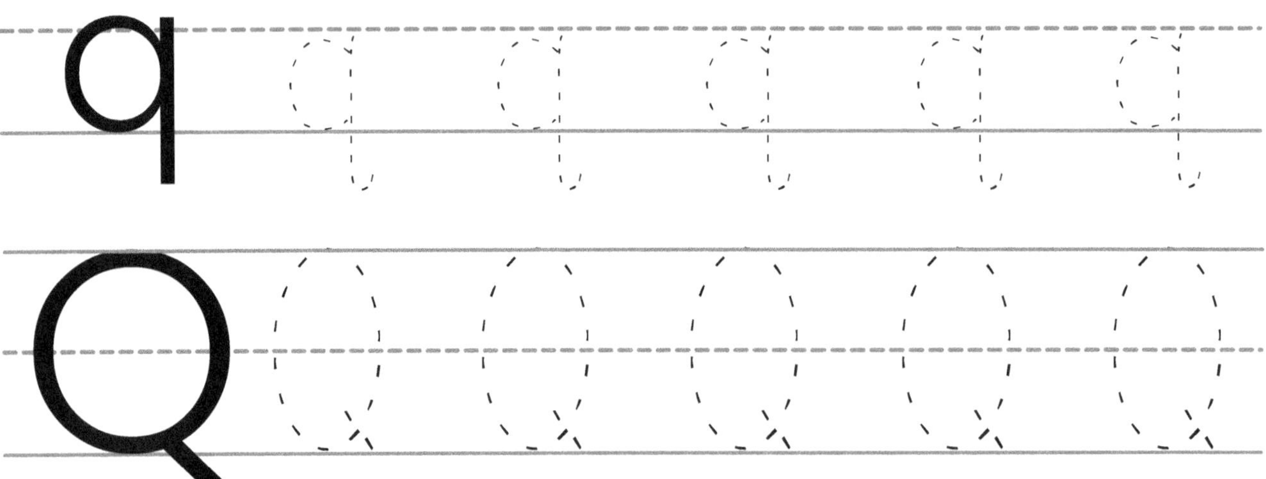

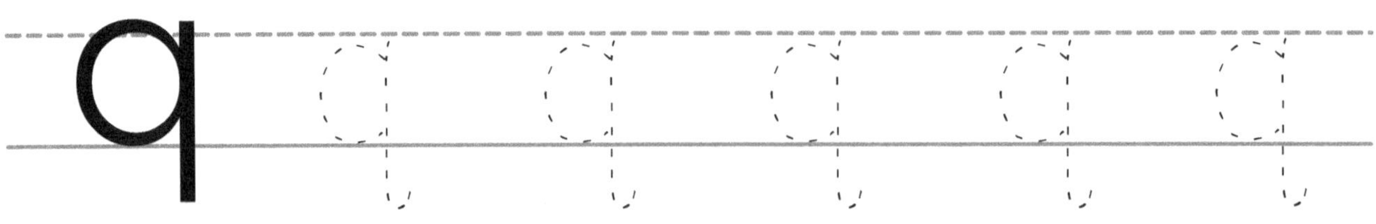

Q
q
Q
q
Q
q

Name:
Date:

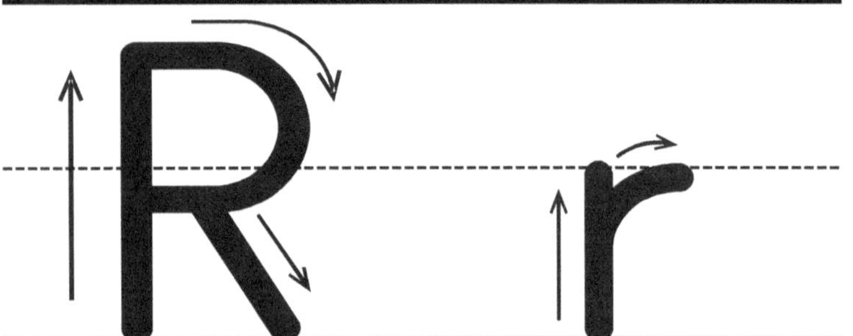

Trace the letters and then practice
writing them on your own!
R r

Rabbit

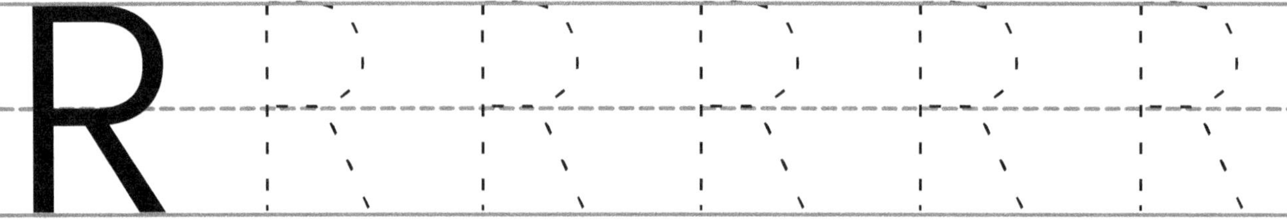

R

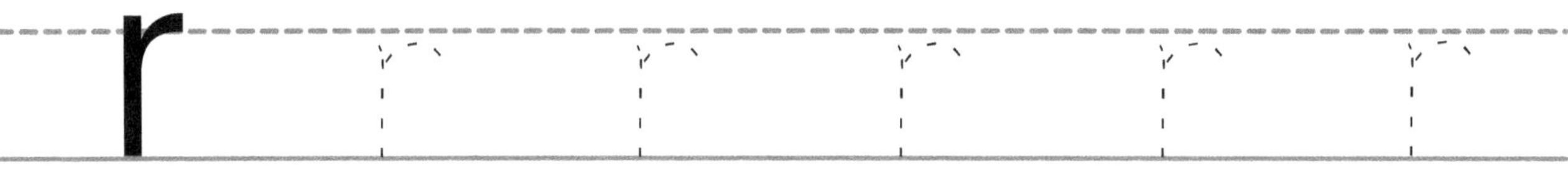

r

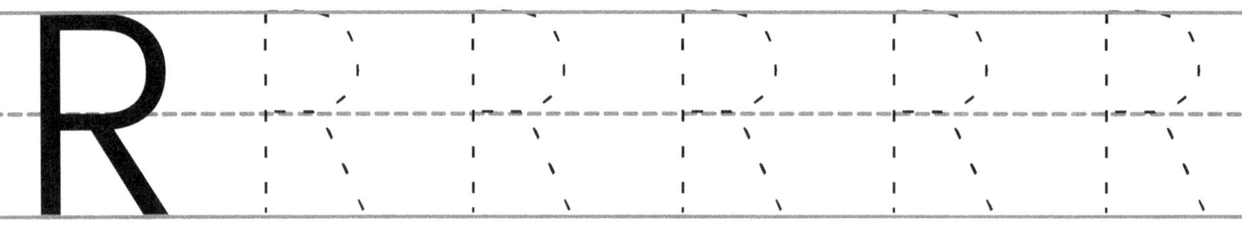

R

r

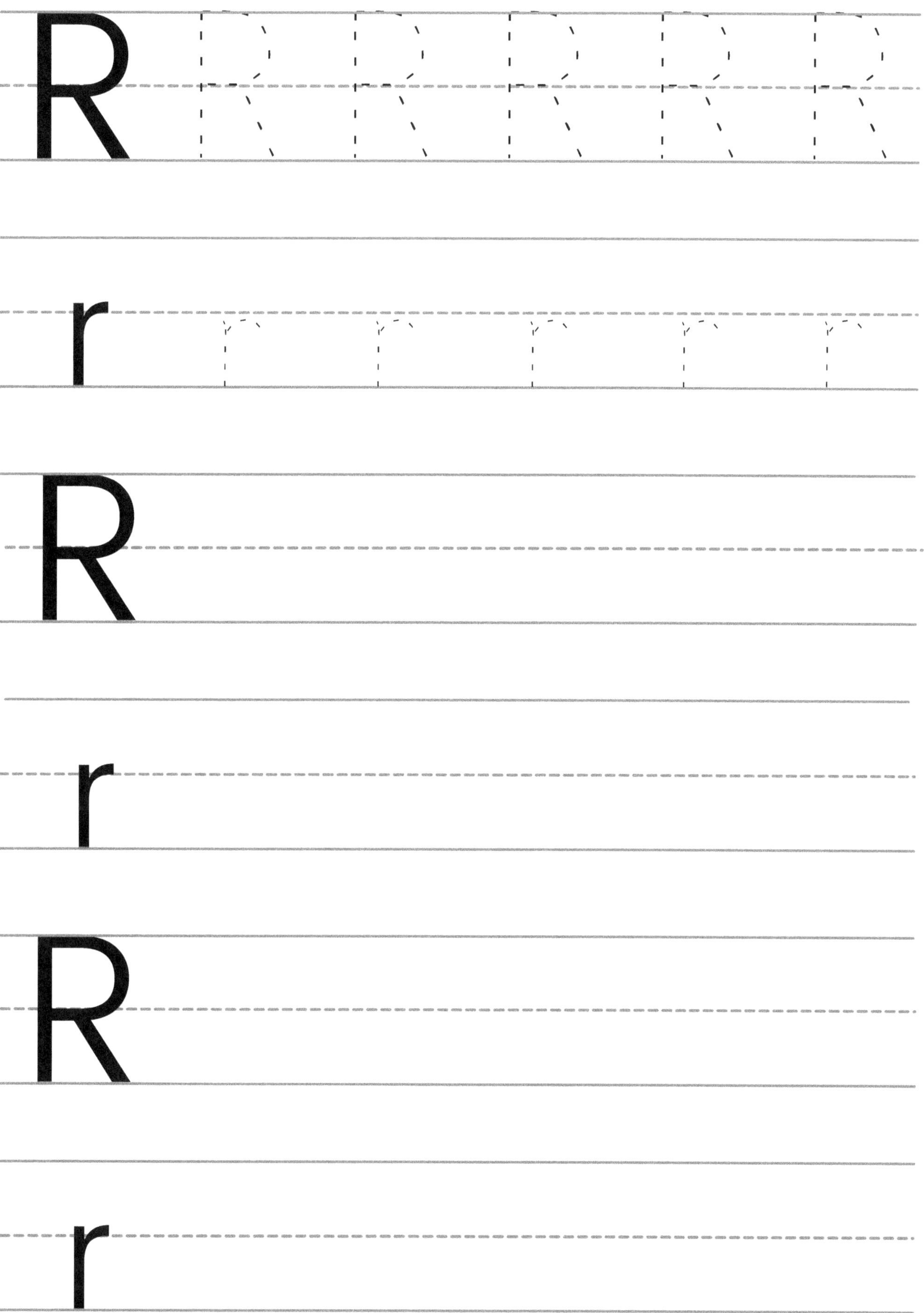

Trace the letters and then practice writing them on your own!

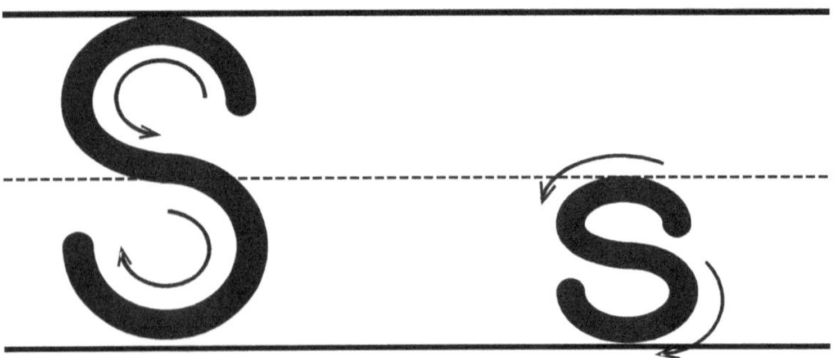

Snail

Trace the letters and then practice writing them on your own!

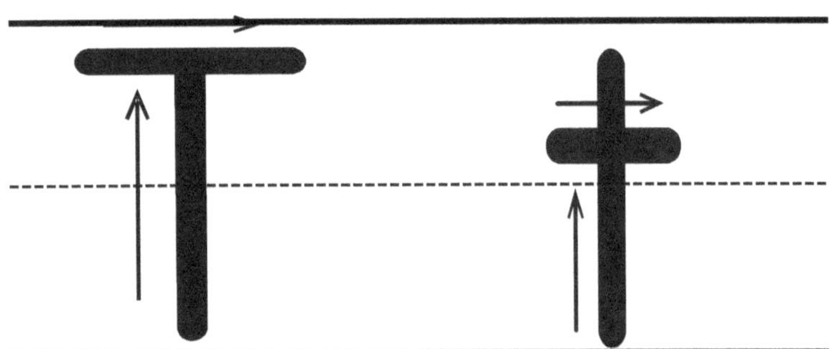

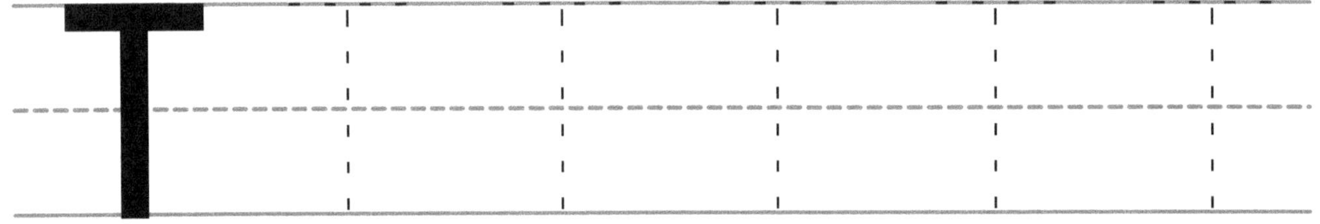

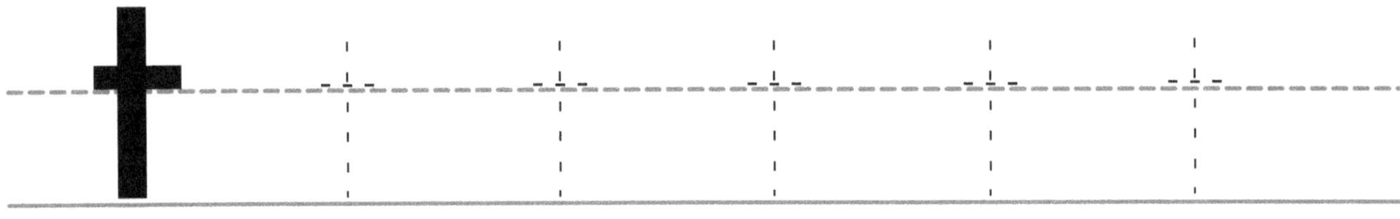

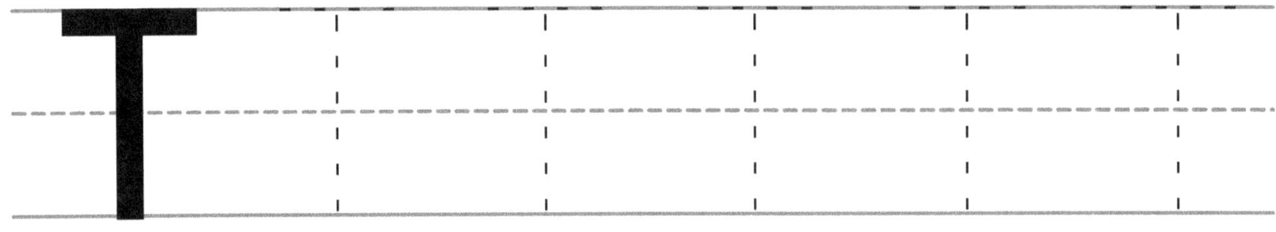

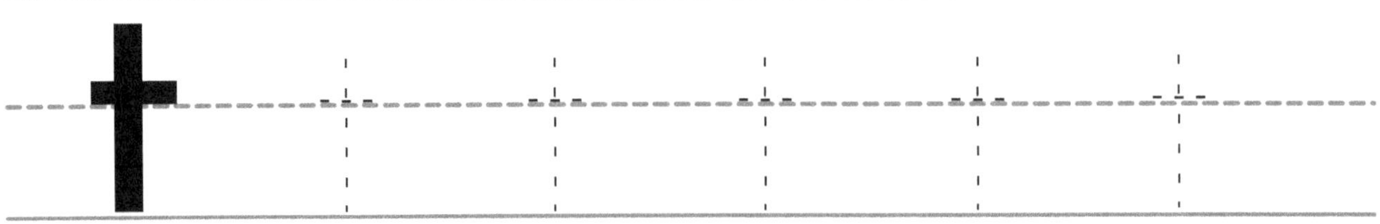

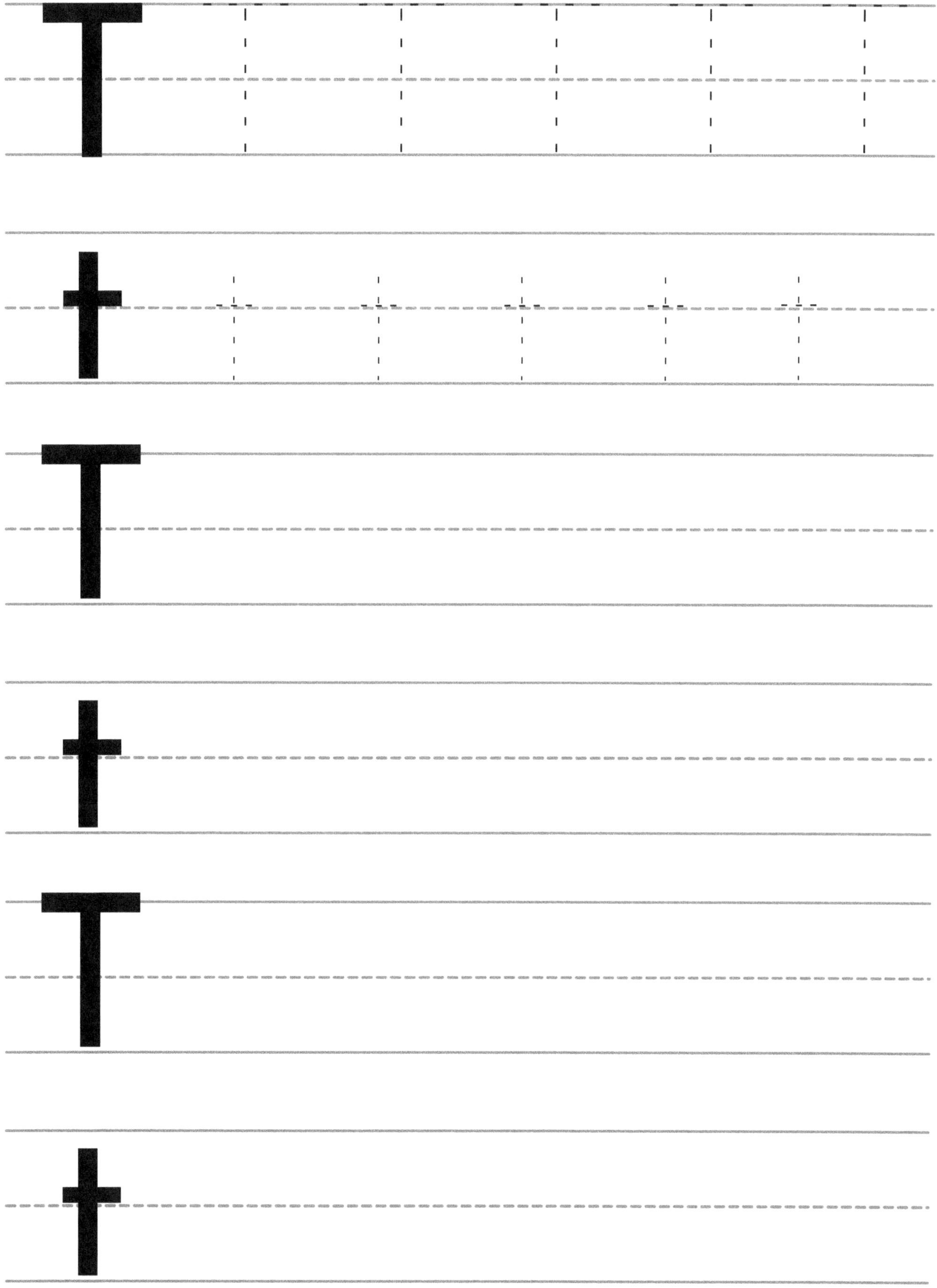

Name: ___________________ Date: ___________________

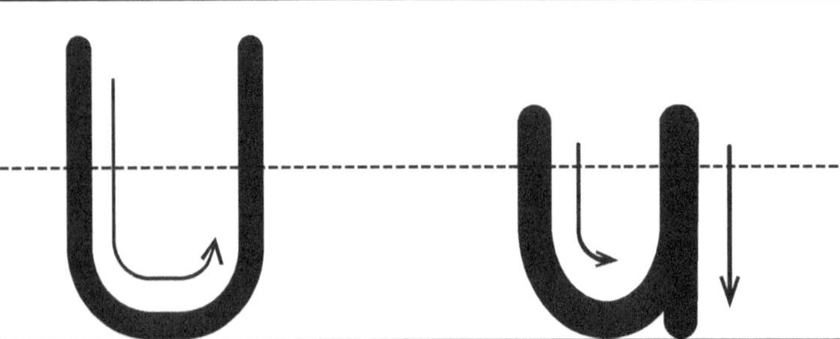

Unicorn

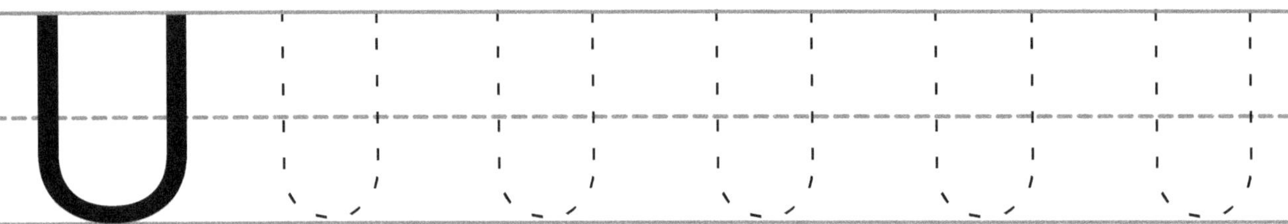

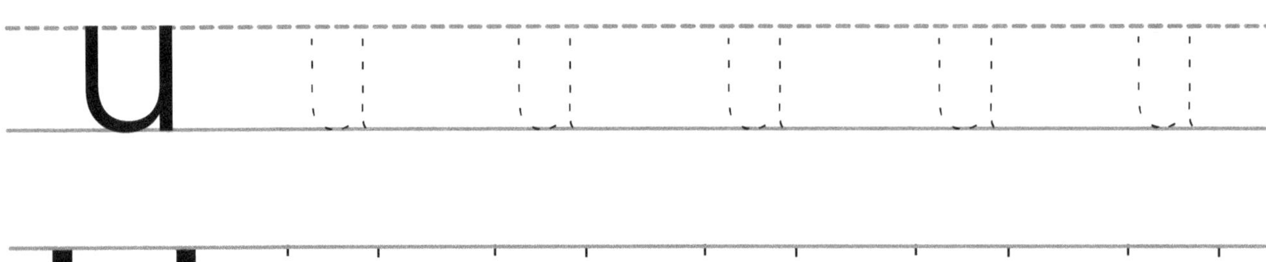

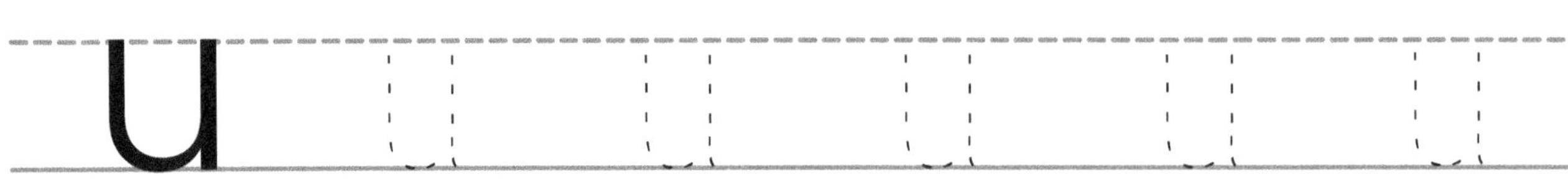

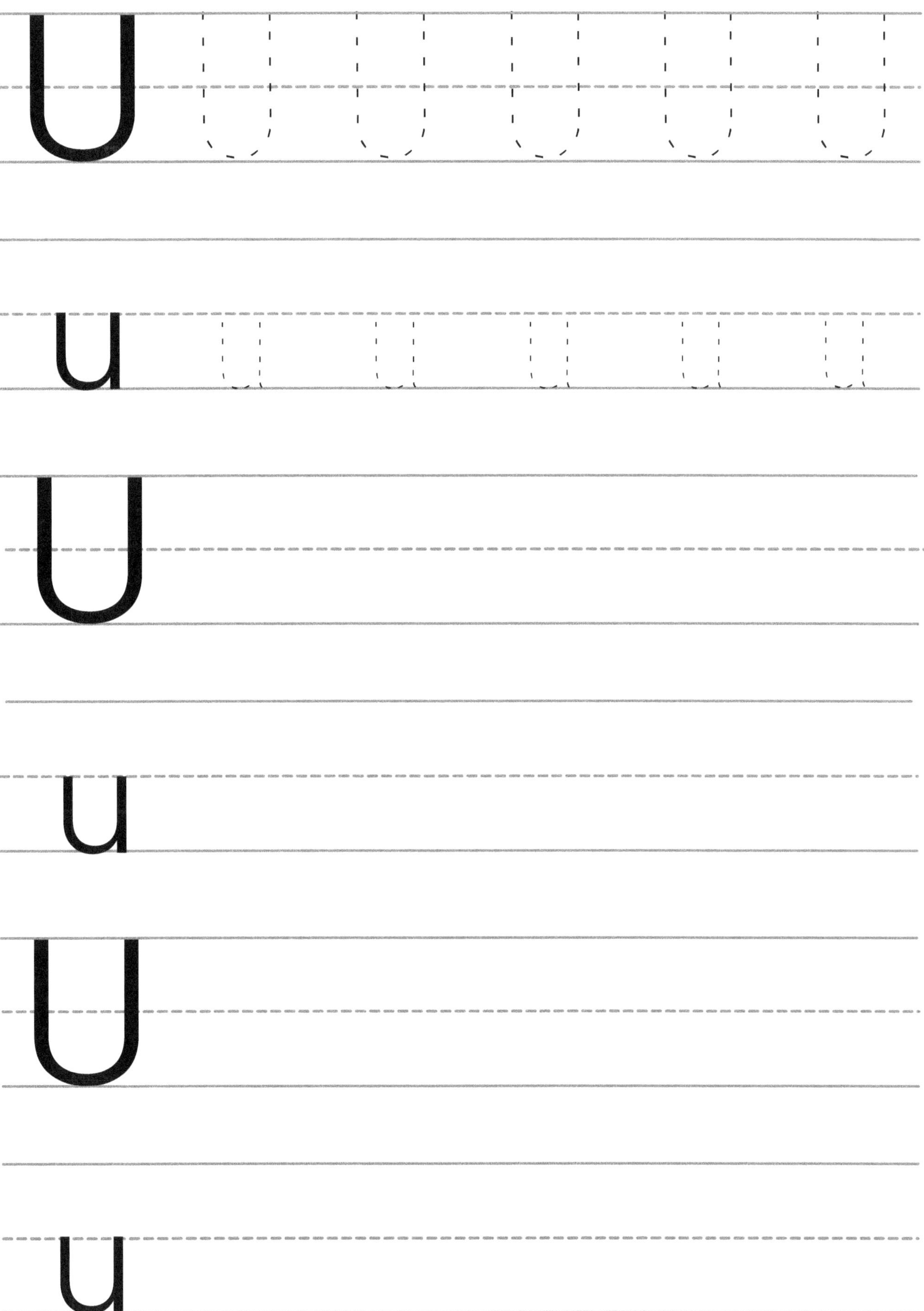

Trace the letters and then practice
writing them on your own!

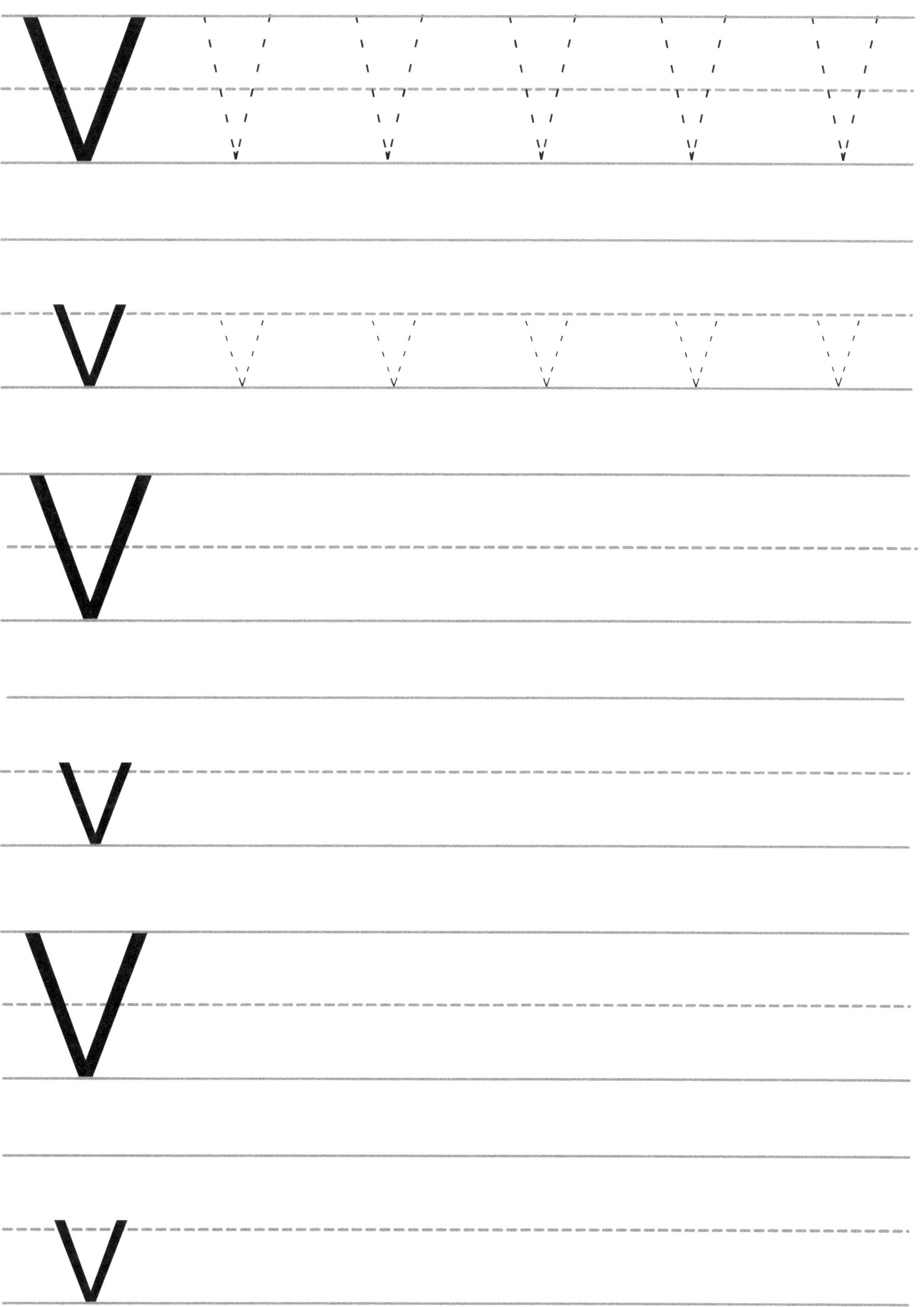

Trace the letters and then practice writing them on your own!

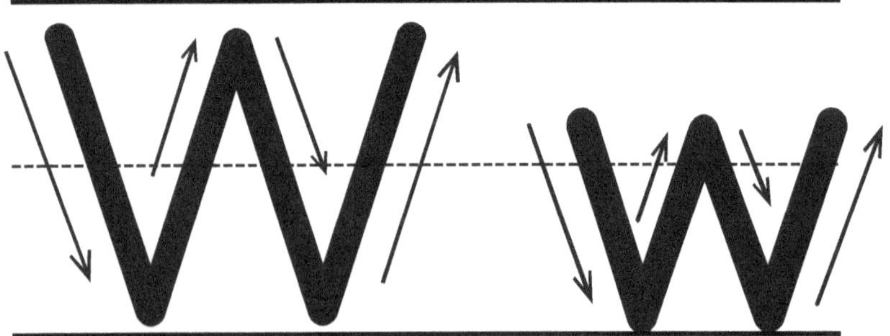

Whale

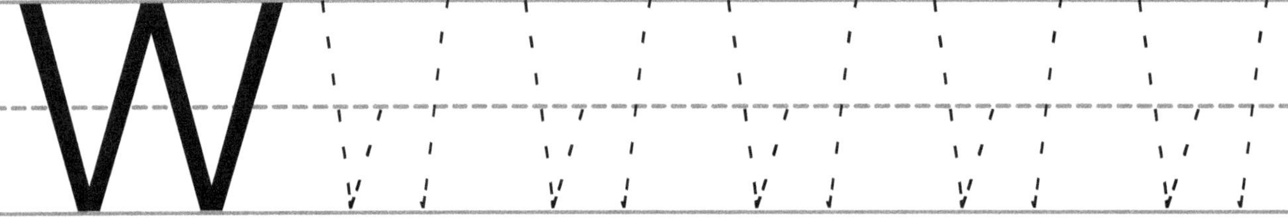

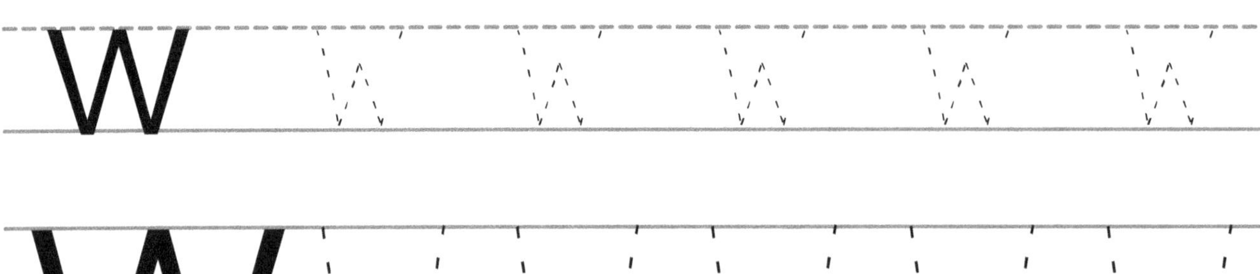

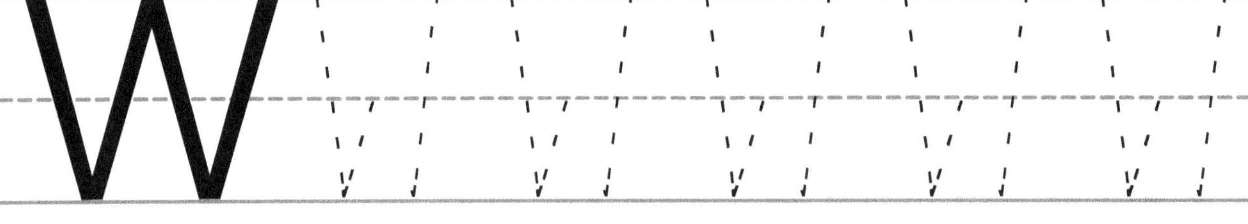

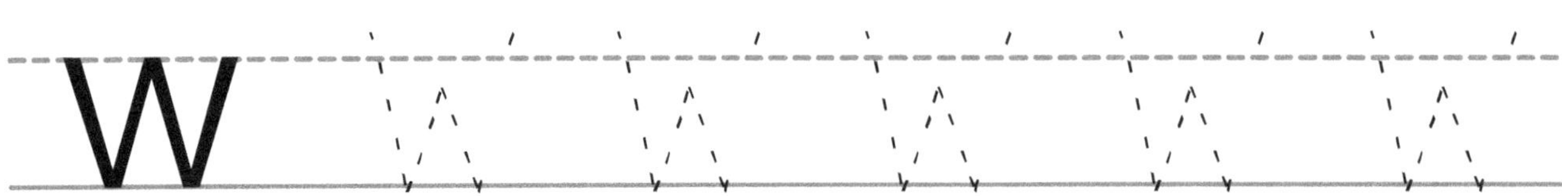

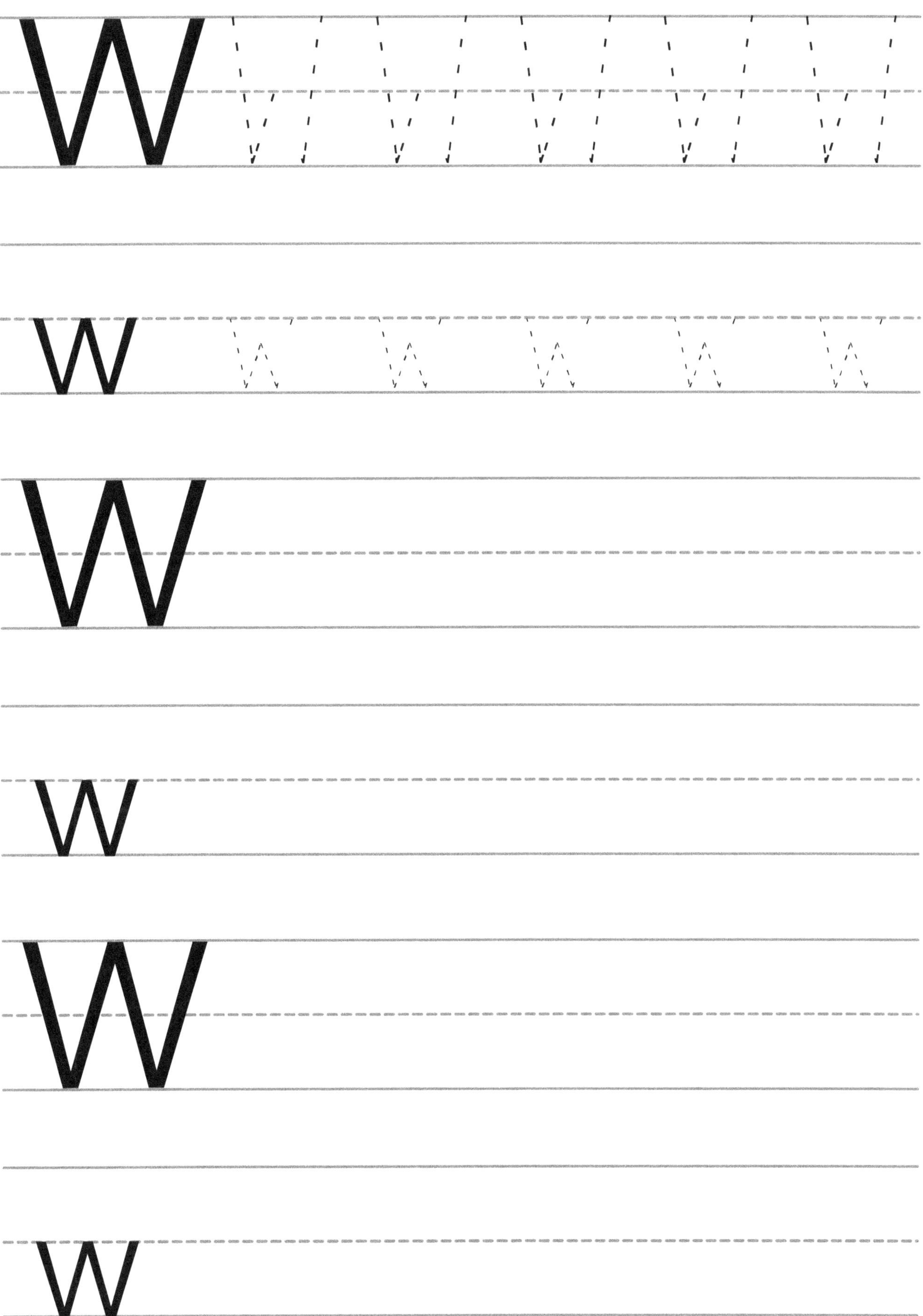

Trace the letters and then practice writing them on your own!

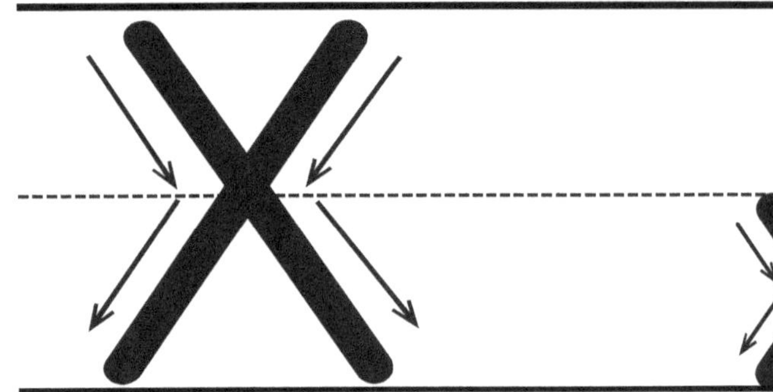

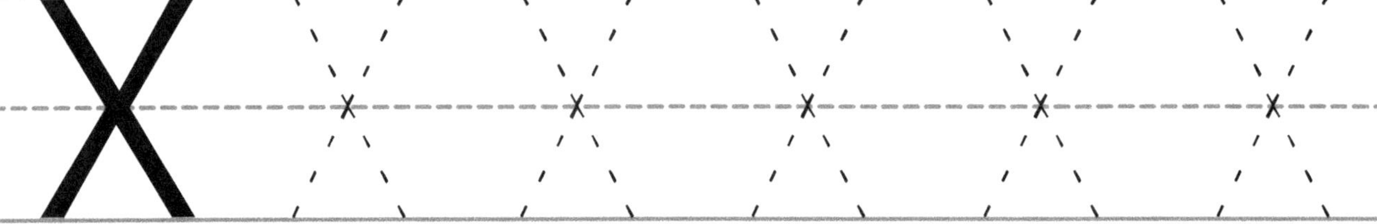

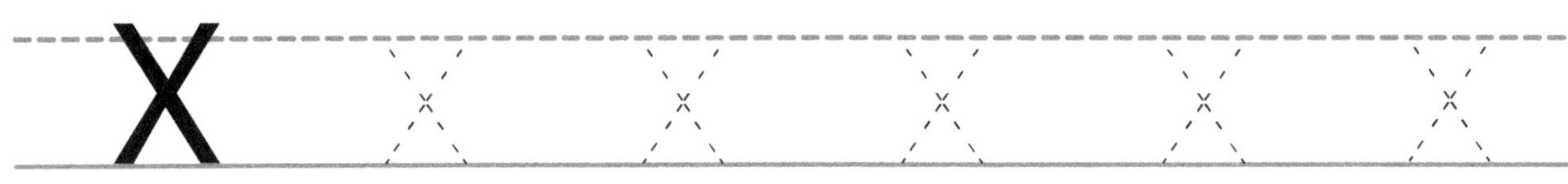

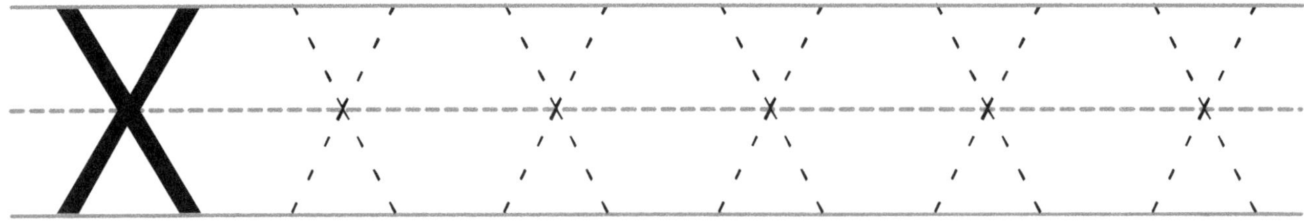

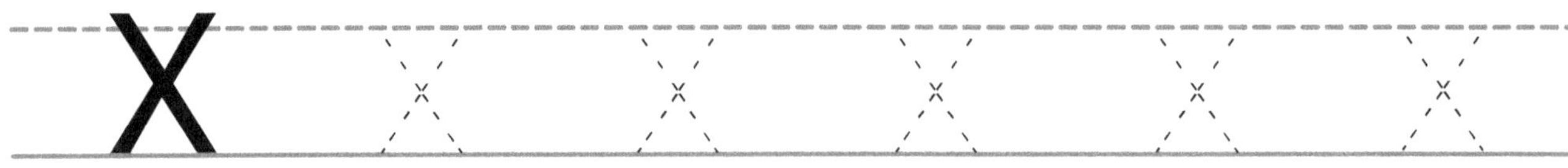

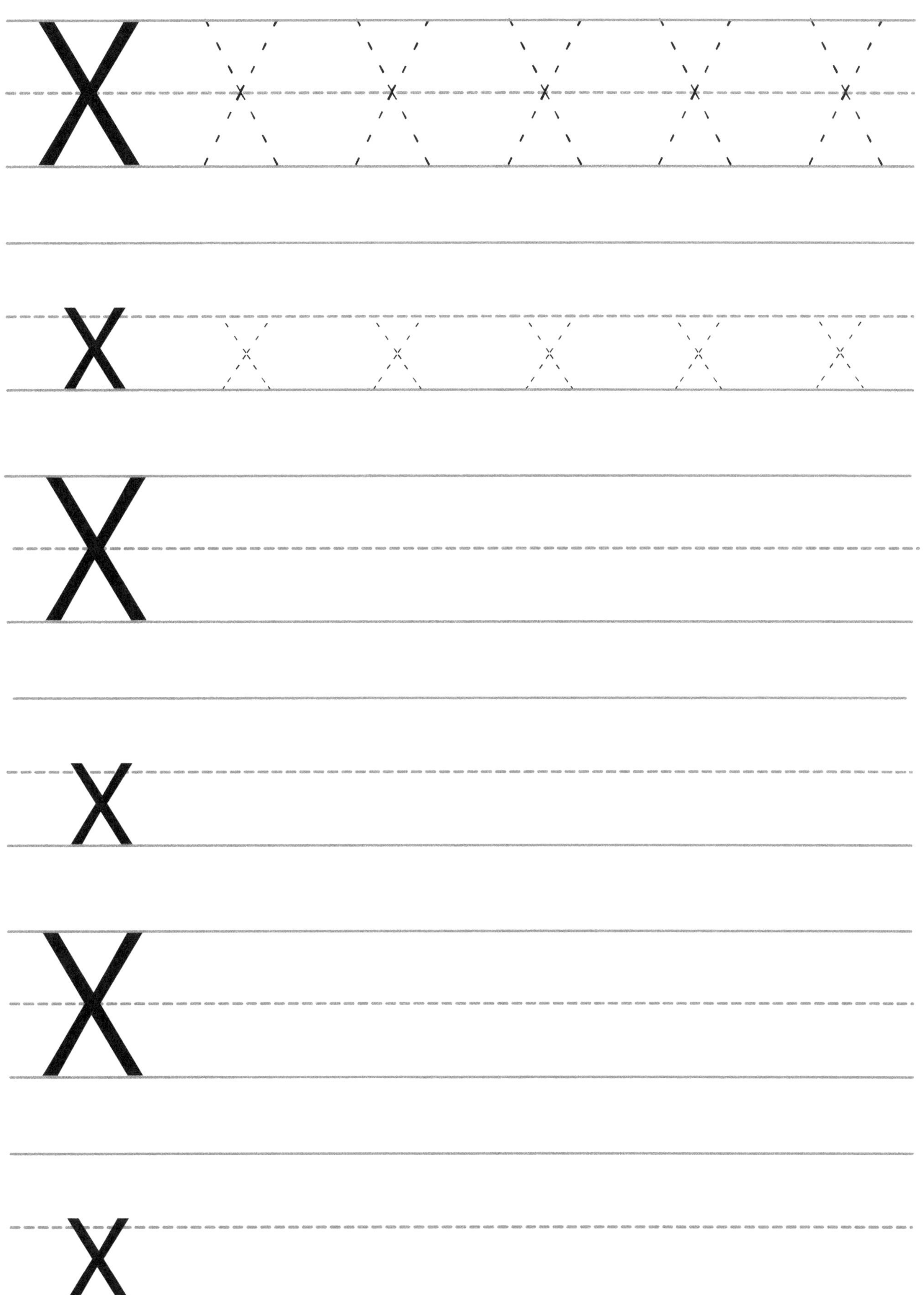

Trace the letters and then practice writing them on your own!

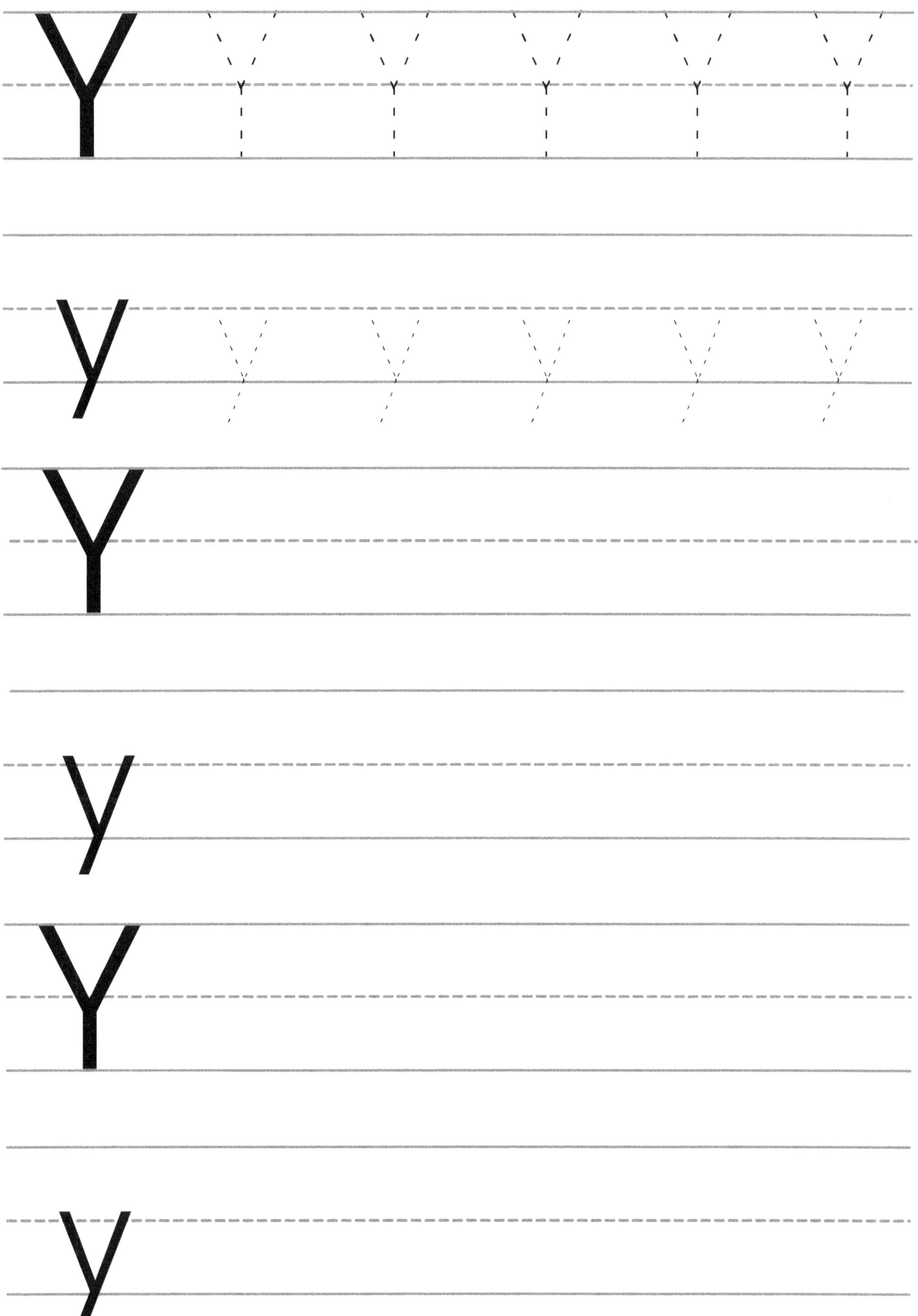

Trace the letters and then practice writing them on your own!

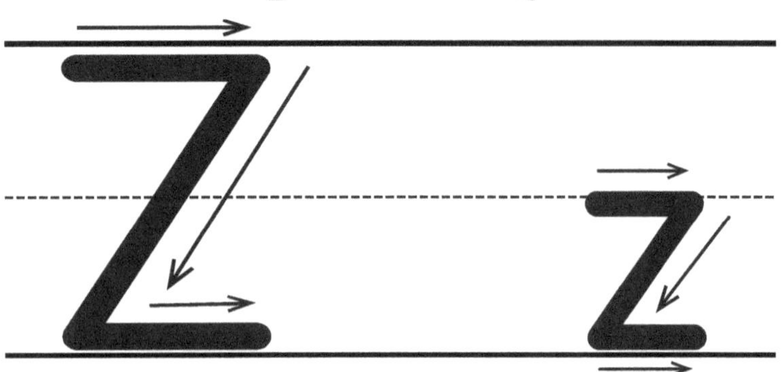

Z

Z

Z

Z

Z

Z

PART 2

Trace and write the sight words!

Find and color the sight words!

and

ask

why

and

me

no

yes

and

not

and

up

 **Trace and write the sight words!**

ant   ant   ant

Find and color the sight words!

and   here   ant   cute

here   look

me   ant   at   be   ant

Name: ___________________

Date: ___________________

 **Trace and write the sight words!**

are are are

 **Find and color the sight words!**

go

his

at him are

are

like me are can

Name: ________________

Date: ________________

 **Trace and write the sight words!**

at   at   at   at

 **Find and color the sight words!**

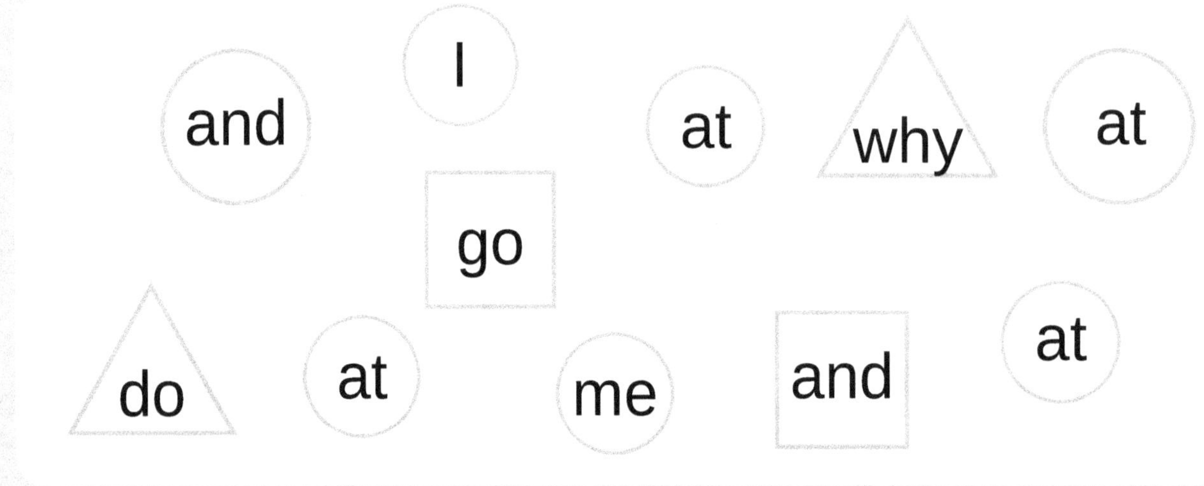

Trace and write the sight words!

Find and color the sight words!

car

fun

the

to

aunt

aunt

aunt

and

at

bike

aunt

 **Trace and write the sight words!**

 **Find and color the sight words!**

 **Trace and write the sight words!**

blue blue blue

 **Find and color the sight words!**

see

can

be blue

for

blue

it blue one blue me

Trace and write the sight words!

Find and color the sight words!

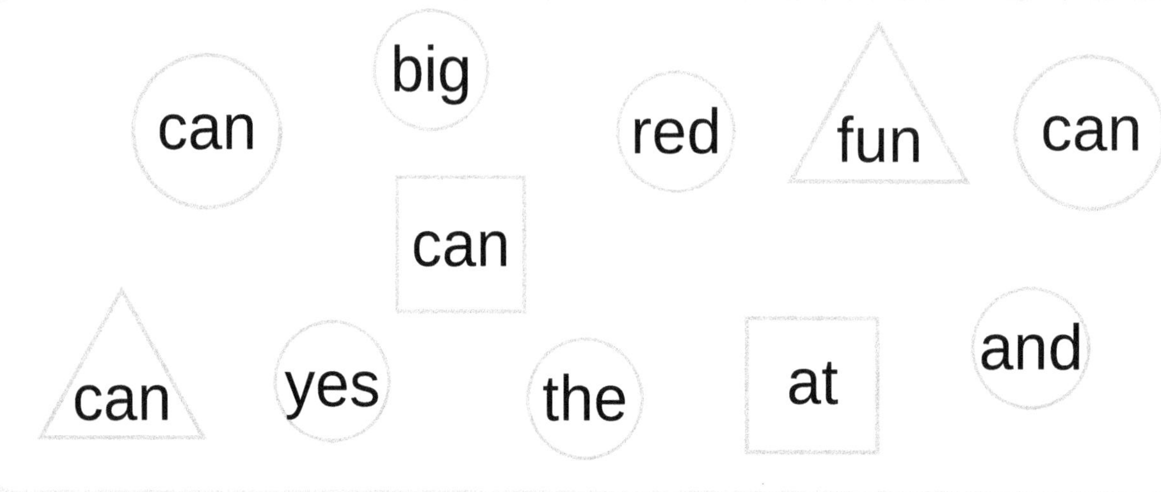

Name: _______________________

Date: _______________________

Trace and write the sight words!

come   come

Find and color the sight words!

see

can

be

for

come

come

it

come

one

come

me

 **Trace and write the sight words!**

down   down

Find and color the sight words!

 **Trace and write the sight words!**

 **Find and color the sight words!**

 **Trace and write the sight words!**

for for for

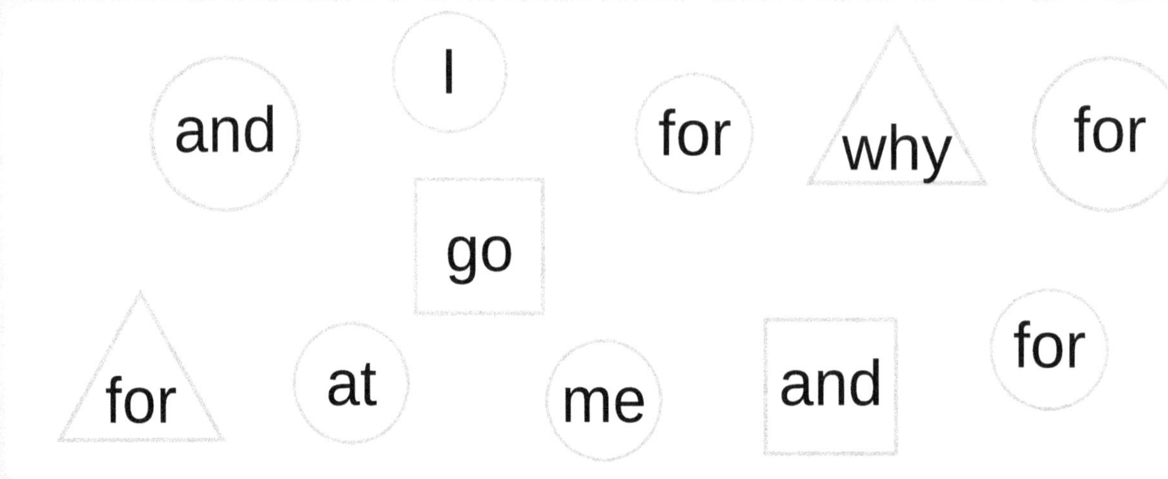 **Find and color the sight words!**

Trace and write the sight words!

Find and color the sight words!

go

his

at   funny   funny

are

funny

like   me   are   can

Trace and write the sight words!

go   go go   go go   go

Find and color the sight words!

Name: ______________________

Date: ______________________

 **Trace and write the sight words!**

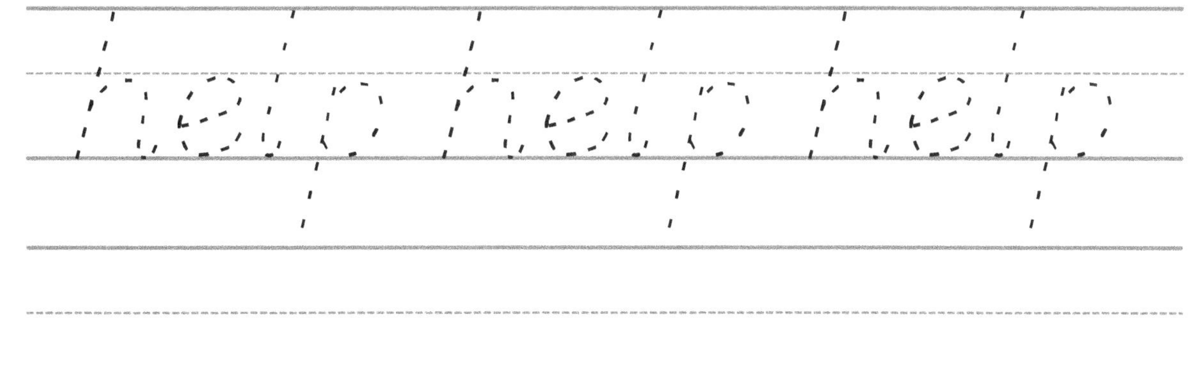

 **Find and color the sight words!**

help

me

here

help

for

and

at

help

blue

help

play

 **Trace and write the sight words!**

here here here

 **Find and color the sight words!**

Trace and write the sight words!

Find and color the sight words!

play

I

why

I

me

no

yes

I

I

and

up

Trace and write the sight words!

Find and color the sight words!

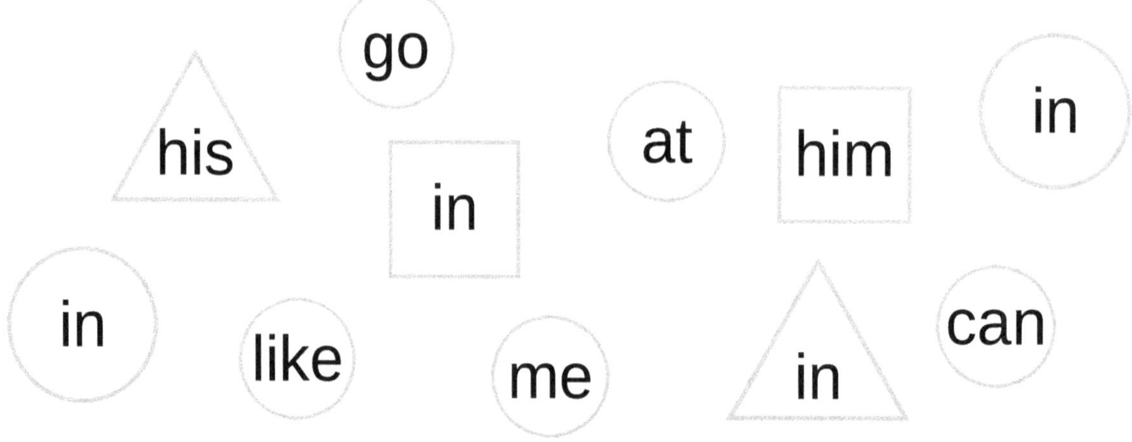

Trace and write the sight words!

Find and color the sight words!

 **Trace and write the sight words!**

 **Find and color the sight words!**

ask

it

why

and

me

no

yes

it

not

it

up

Name: _______________

Date: _______________

Trace and write the sight words!

jump   jump

Find and color the sight words!

see

jump

eye

and

jump

be

jump

and

run

and

jump

 **Trace and write the sight words!**

 **Find and color the sight words!**

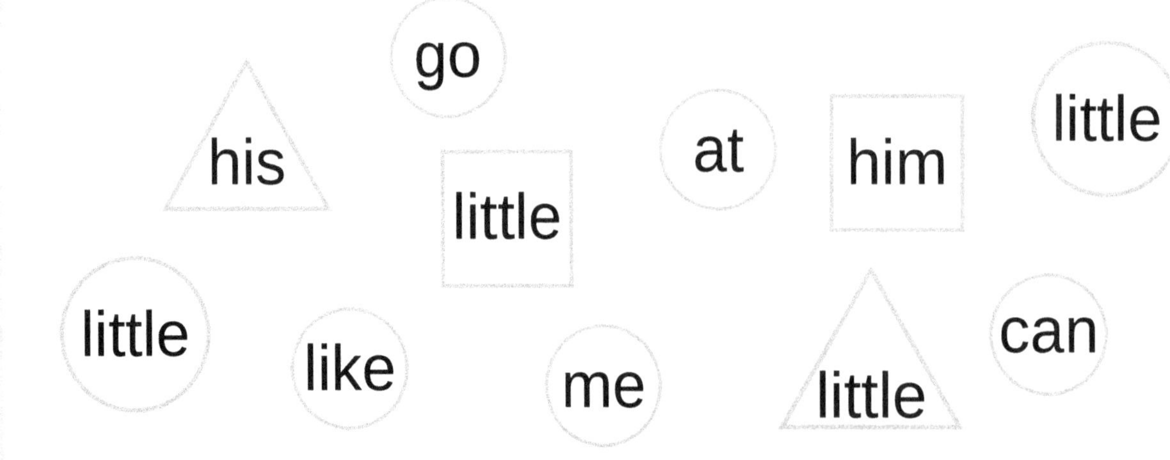

Name: ___________________

Date: ___________________

 **Trace and write the sight words!**

 **Find and color the sight words!**

boy
look
girl
look
look
ten
the
look
say
look
me

Name: ___________

Date: ___________

Trace and write the sight words!

make make

Find and color the sight words!

make ask why make me

no

yes make not make up

Trace and write the sight words!

me me me me

Find and color the sight words!

and

I

me why me

go

do me me and me

Trace and write the sight words!

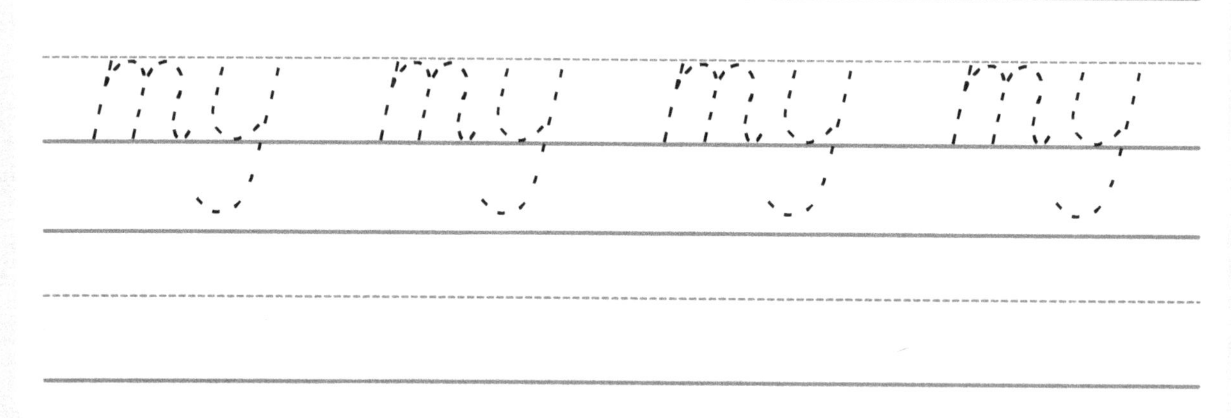

Find and color the sight words!

 **Trace and write the sight words!**

not not not not not

 **Find and color the sight words!**

go

his

at

him

not

not

not

like

me

not

can

 **Trace and write the sight words!**

Find and color the sight words!

Trace and write the sight words!

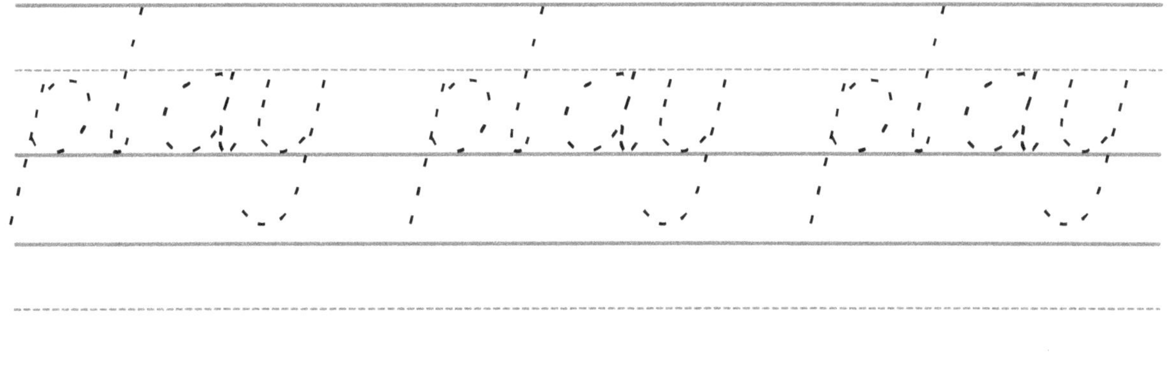

Find and color the sight words!

Name: _______________

Date: _______________

 **Trace and write the sight words!**

 **Find and color the sight words!**

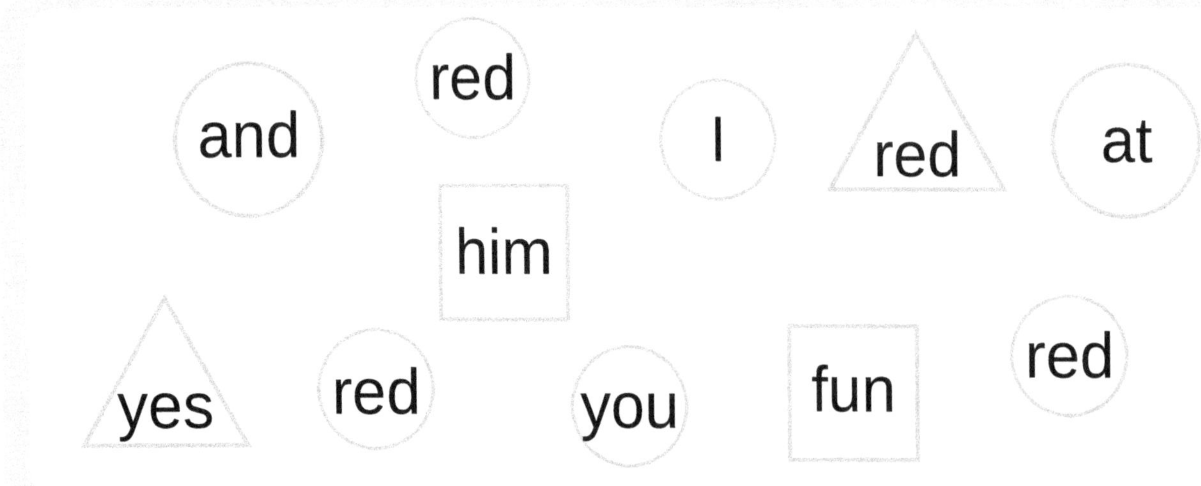

Trace and write the sight words!

run   run   run

Find and color the sight words!

l

run

run   why   run

go

do   run   me   and   run

Name:

Date:

 **Trace and write the sight words!**

 **Find and color the sight words!**

go

his

sad

at

sad

sad

sad

like

me

are

can

Name: ________________

Date: ________________

Trace and write the sight words!

see   see   see

Find and color the sight words!

see   two   him   and   are

see   see   like

at   to   me   and   can

 **Trace and write the sight words!**

 **Find and color the sight words!**

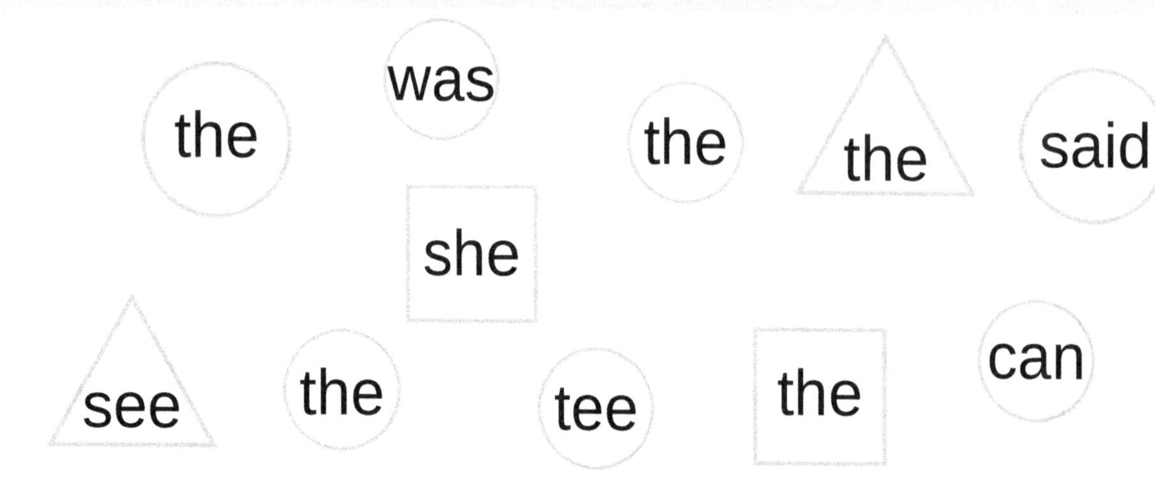

Trace and write the sight words!

three three

Find and color the sight words!

three

me

go

four

three

and

three

but

can

yes

three

 **Trace and write the sight words!**

to to to to to

Find and color the sight words!

and

to

to

why

to

go

do

to

me

and

to

Trace and write the sight words!

Find and color the sight words!

two

all

be

two

two

bee

two

make

one

and

at

Trace and write the sight words!

up   up   up   up

Find and color the sight words!

go

his

said

at

said

said

said

like

me

are

can

 **Trace and write the sight words!**

we   we   we   we

 **Find and color the sight words!**

and   here   we   cute

here   look

me   we   at   we   we

Name: _______________________

Date: _______________________

Trace and write the sight words!

where   where

Find and color the sight words!

where   me   go   four

where   and

where   but   can   yes   where

Trace and write the sight words!

yellow   yellow

Find and color the sight words!

to

yellow   out   and   yellow

yellow

big   and   me   and   up

Name:

Date:

Trace and write the sight words!

you you you

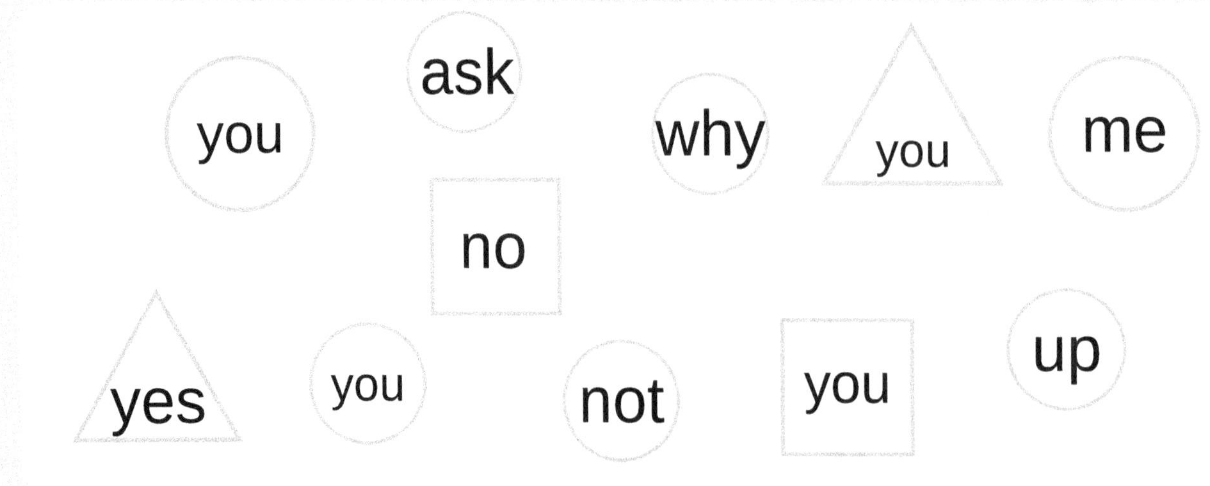

Find and color the sight words!

Name: ___________________

Date: ___________________

 **Trace and write the sight words!**

xylophone

 **Find and color the sight words!**

ask

xylophone

why

xylophone

me

xylophone

no

yes

not

you

up

Name: _______________________

Date: _______________________

 **Trace and write the sight words!**

zoo   zoo   zoo

Find and color the sight words!

ask

zoo

why   zoo   me

no

yes   zoo   not   zoo   up

PART 3

I love mom and dad.

Trace the sentence!

Practice writing the sentence!

Name: _______________________

Date: _______________________

The ant is small.

Trace the sentence!

The ant is small.

The ant is small.

Practice writing the sentence!

Name: _________________

Date: _________________

 **Trace the sentence!**

You are a boy.

You are a boy.

 **Practice writing the sentence!**

I am at home.

Trace the sentence!

I am at home.

I am at home.

Practice writing the sentence!

She is my aunt.

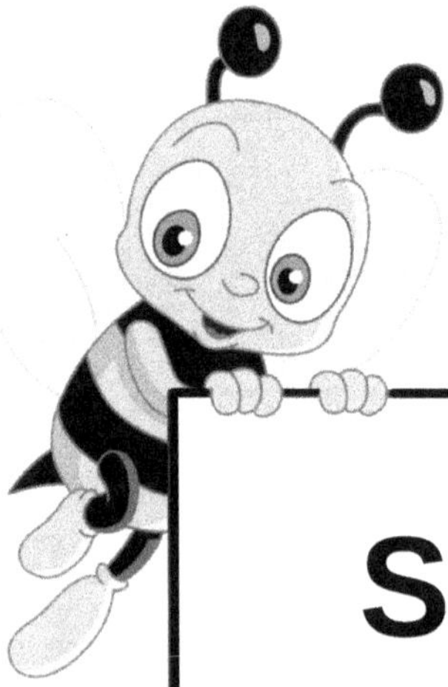

She is my aunt.

She is my aunt.

I see a big plane.

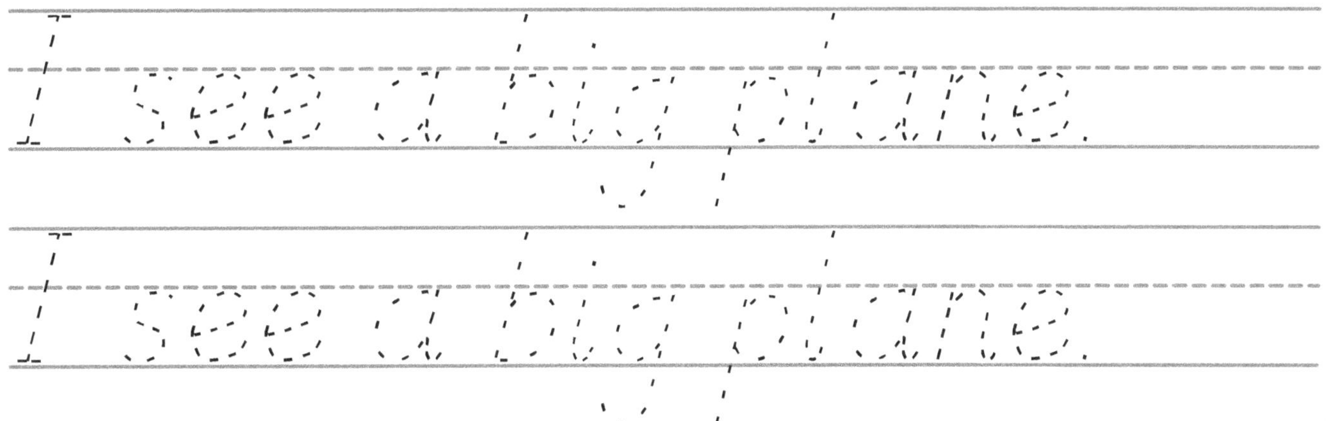

Trace the sentence!

I see a big plane.

I see a big plane.

Practice writing the sentence!

Name: _______________________

Date: _______________________

The sky is blue.

 **Trace the sentence!**

The sky is blue.

The sky is blue.

 **Practice writing the sentence!**

Name: _______________________

Date: _______________________

I can write.

Trace the sentence!

I can write.

I can write.

Practice writing the sentence!

Name: _______________________

Date: _______________________

I come to play.

Trace the sentence!

I come to play.

I come to play.

Practice writing the sentence!

I sit at the table.

I sit at the table.

I sit at the table.

Let's find the dog!

Trace the sentence!

Practice writing the sentence!

Name: _______________

Date: _______________

The gift is for me.

Trace the sentence!

The gift is for me.

The gift is for me.

Practice writing the sentence!

Name: _______________

Date: _______________

I am funny.

 **Trace the sentence!**

I am funny.

I am funny.

Practice writing the sentence!

Name: _______________

Date: _______________

I go to the park.

 **Trace the sentence!**

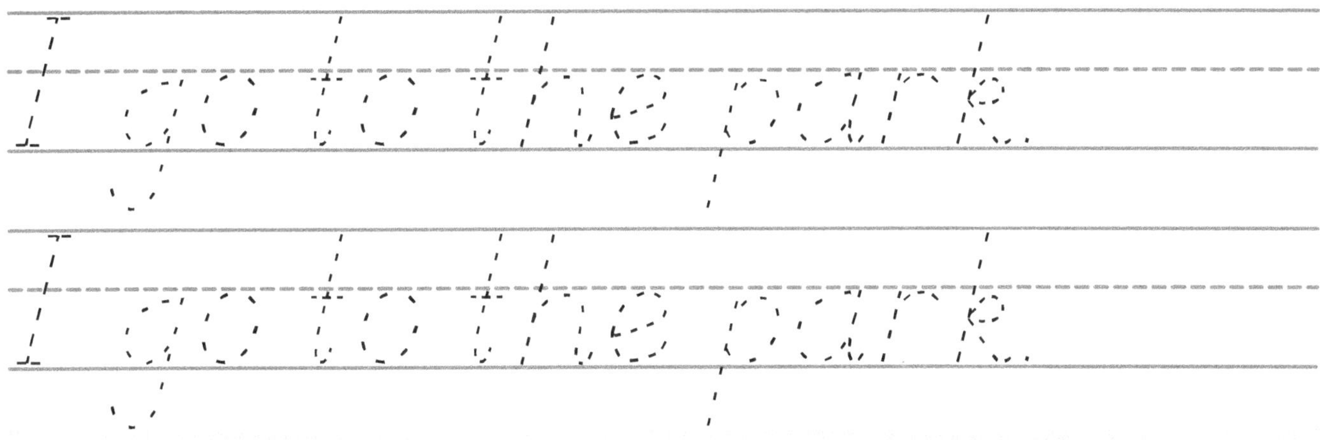

Practice writing the sentence!

Name: _______________________

Date: _______________________

I help mom to cook.

Trace the sentence!

I help mom to cook.

I help mom to cook.

Practice writing the sentence!

Name: ___________________

Date: ___________________

The cat is here.

 **Trace the sentence!**

The cat is here.

The cat is here.

 **Practice writing the sentence!**

I like to draw.

 **Trace the sentence!**

I like to draw.

I like to draw.

 **Practice writing the sentence!**

I live in a house.

Trace the sentence!

I live in a house.

I live in a house.

Practice writing the sentence!

Name: _______________

Date: _______________

The elephant is big.

Trace the sentence!

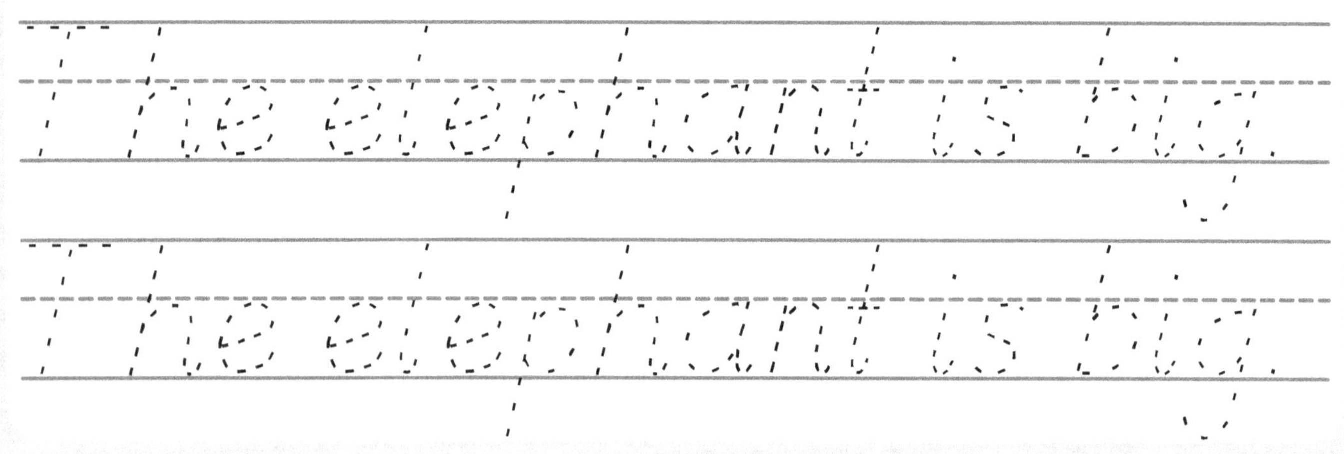

Practice writing the sentence!

Name: ___________________

Date: ___________________

It is sunny outside.

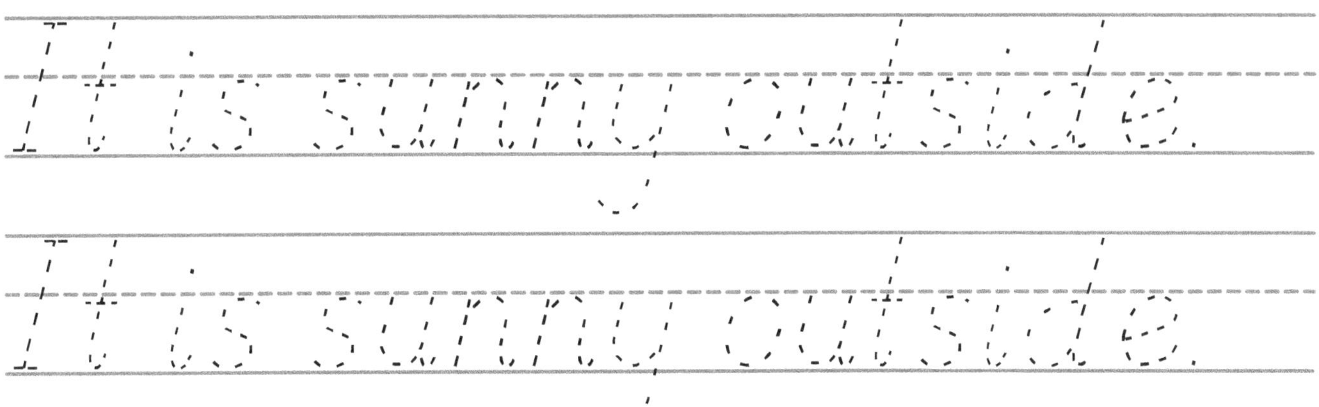

Trace the sentence!

It is sunny outside.

It is sunny outside.

Practice writing the sentence!

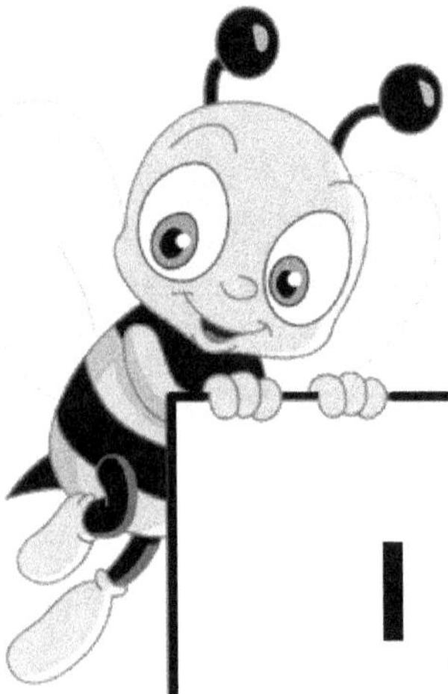

I jump so high!

Trace the sentence!

I jump so high!
I jump so high!

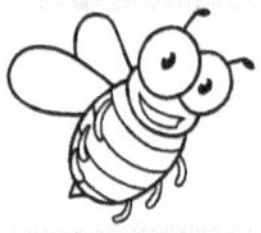

Practice writing the sentence!

Name: _______________________

Date: _______________________

I am little.

I am little.

I am little.

Name: _______________________

Date: _______________________

Look at the birds.

Look at the birds.

Look at the birds.

Name: _______________

Date: _______________

I make cupcakes.

 **Trace the sentence!**

I make cupcakes.

I make cupcakes.

Practice writing the sentence!

Name: _______________

Date: _______________

The dog likes me.

 **Trace the sentence!**

 **Practice writing the sentence!**

My name is Buzzy.

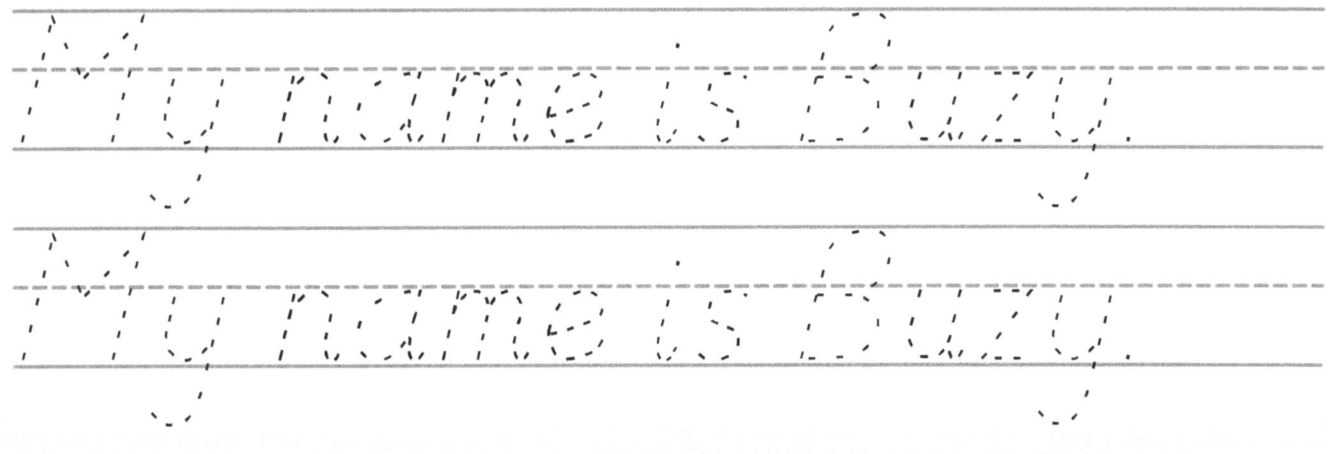

Practice writing the sentence!

Name: ___________________

Date: ___________________

It is not my hat.

Trace the sentence!

It is not my hat.

It is not my hat.

Practice writing the sentence!

Name: _______________________

Date: _______________________

I have one book.

Trace the sentence!

I have one book.

I have one book.

Practice writing the sentence!

Name: ___________________

Date: ___________________

I play with my toys.

Trace the sentence!

I play with my toys.

I play with my toys.

Practice writing the sentence!

Name:

Date:

This dress is red.

 **Trace the sentence!**

This dress is red.

This dress is red.

 **Practice writing the sentence!**

I run the fastest.

Trace the sentence!

Practice writing the sentence!

Name: ___________________

Date: ___________________

My sister is sad.

Trace the sentence!

My sister is sad.
My sister is sad.

Practice writing the sentence!

Can you see me?

Trace the sentence!

Practice writing the sentence!

The cake is for you.

The cake is for you.

The cake is for you.

I see three bees.

 **Trace the sentence!**

I see three bees.
I see three bees.

 **Practice writing the sentence!**

Name: _______________________

Date: _______________________

I go to the beach.

 **Trace the sentence!**

I go to the beach.

I go to the beach.

 **Practice writing the sentence!**

Name: _______________

Date: _______________

Two birds live here.

 **Trace the sentence!**

Two birds live here.

Two birds live here.

 **Practice writing the sentence!**

Name: _______________________

Date: _______________________

I look up at the sky.

Trace the sentence!

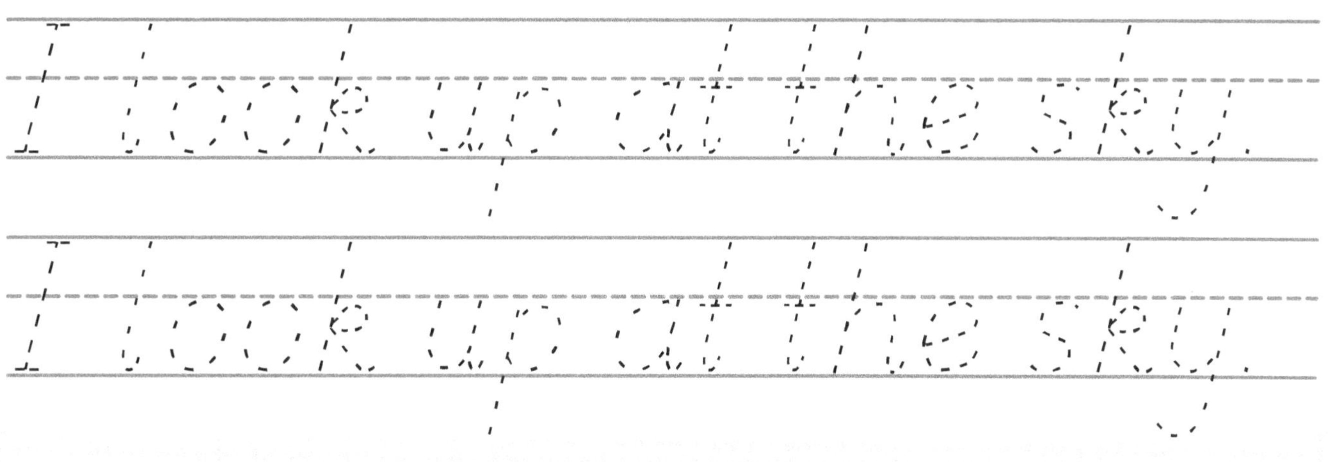

Practice writing the sentence!

Name: _______________

Date: _______________

We eat ice cream.

Trace the sentence!

We eat ice cream.

We eat ice cream.

Practice writing the sentence!

Name: ___________________

Date: ___________________

Where do you live?

Trace the sentence!

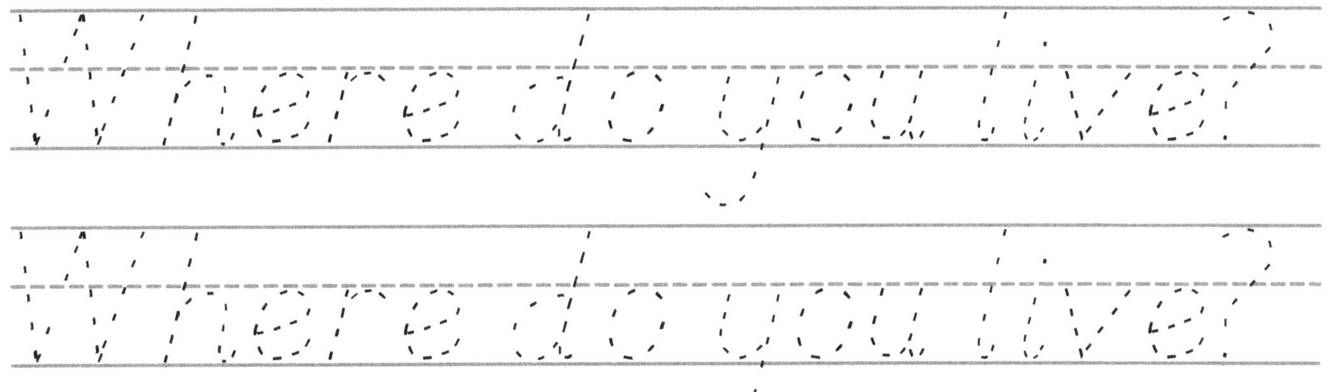

Practice writing the sentence!

Name: _______________________

Date: _______________________

The pencil is yellow.

 **Trace the sentence!**

The pencil is yellow.

The pencil is yellow.

 **Practice writing the sentence!**

You make me smile.

 **Trace the sentence!**

You make me smile.

You make me smile.

 **Practice writing the sentence!**

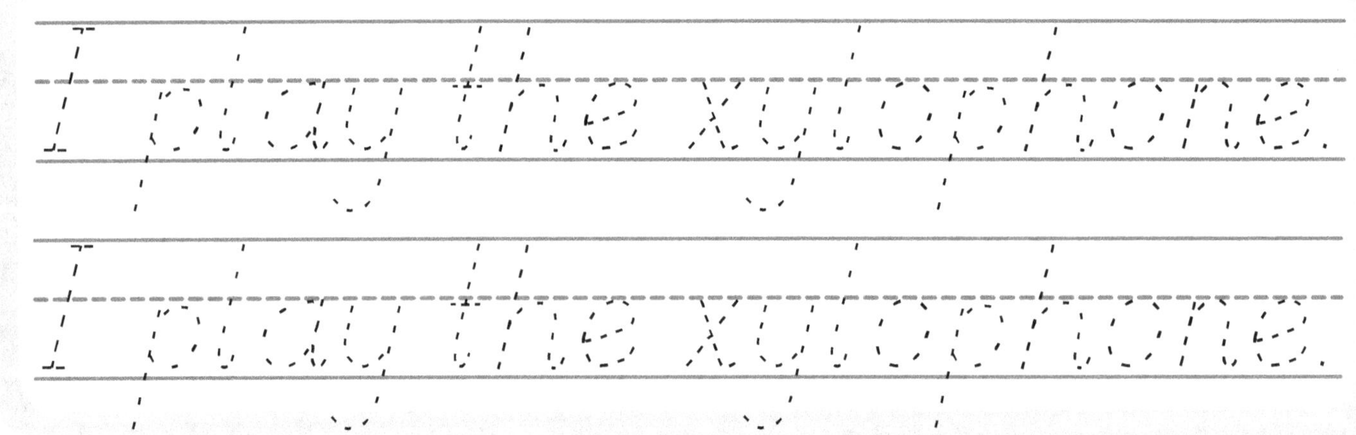

Trace the sentence!

I play the xylophone.

I play the xylophone.

Practice writing the sentence!

Trace the sentence!

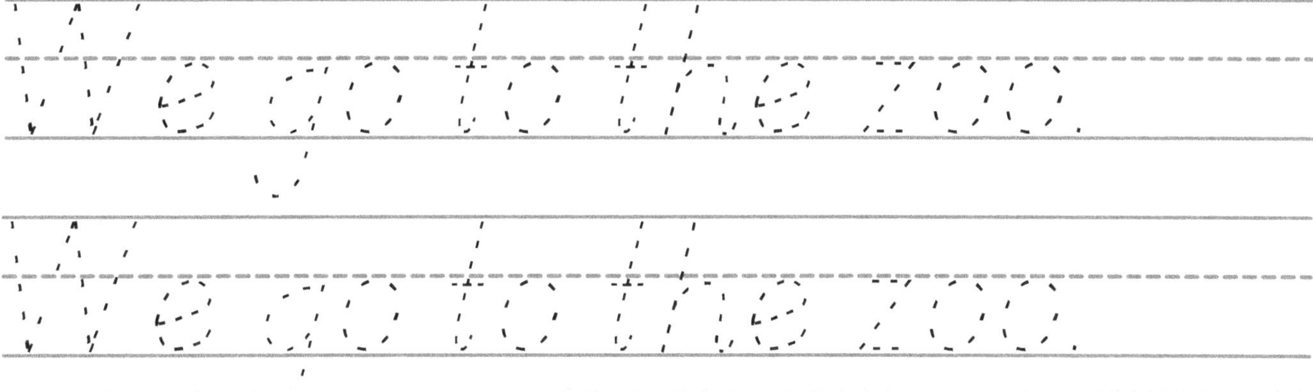

Practice writing the sentence!

PART 4

Name:

Date:

Trace the numbers and then practice writing them on your own in the remaining space!

1 1 1 1 1

2 2 2 2

3 3 3

4 4 4

5 5 5

Name:

Date:

Trace the numbers and then practice writing them on your own in the remaining space!

6 6 6 6

7 7 7 7

8 8 8 8

8 9 9 9

10 10 10 10

Name:

Date:

Trace the numbers and then practice writing them on your own in the remaining space!

11

12

13

14

15

Name: ________________________

Date: ________________________

Trace the numbers and then practice writing them on your own in the remaining space!

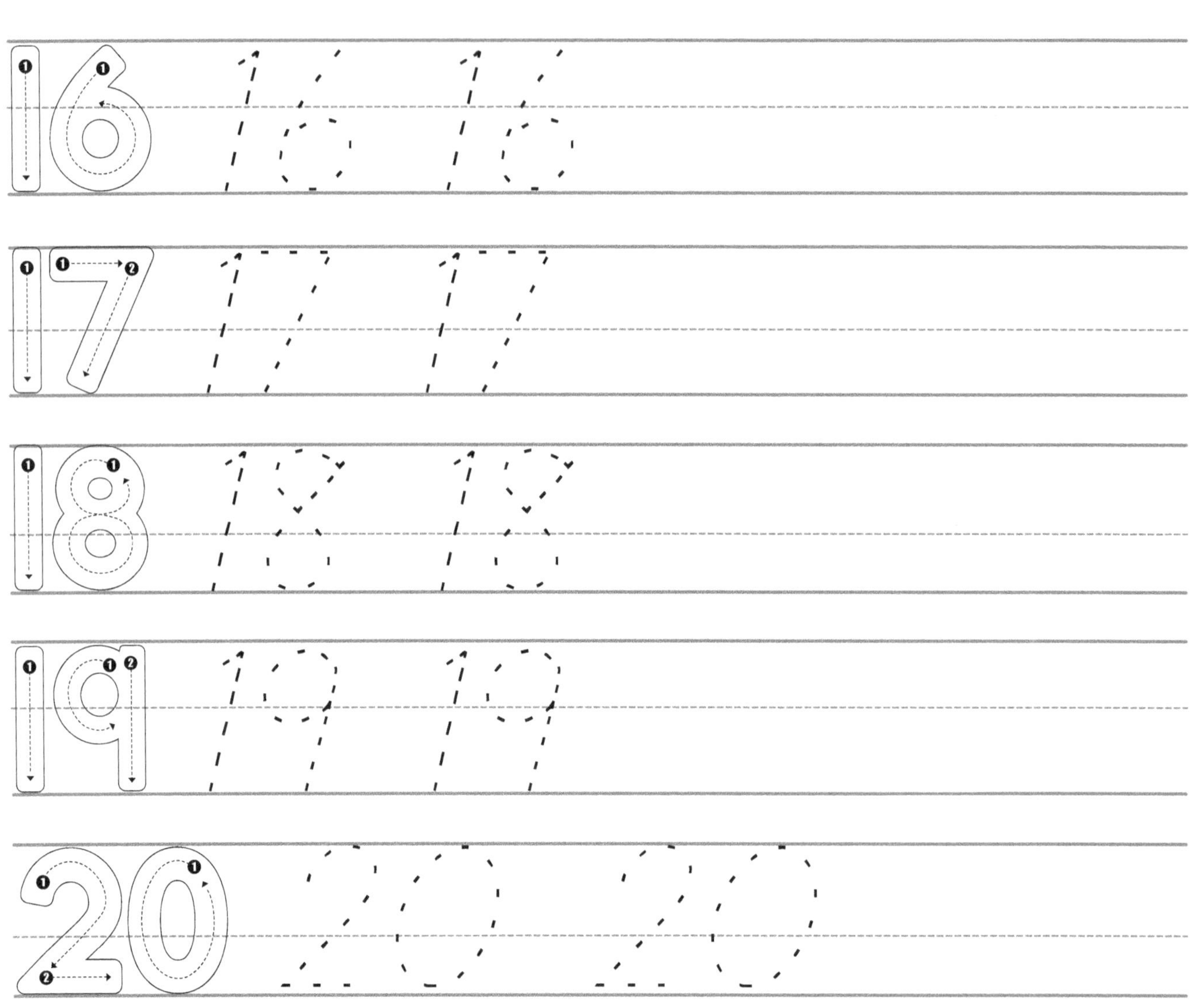

Name:

Date:

Trace the numbers and then practice writing them on your own in the remaining space!

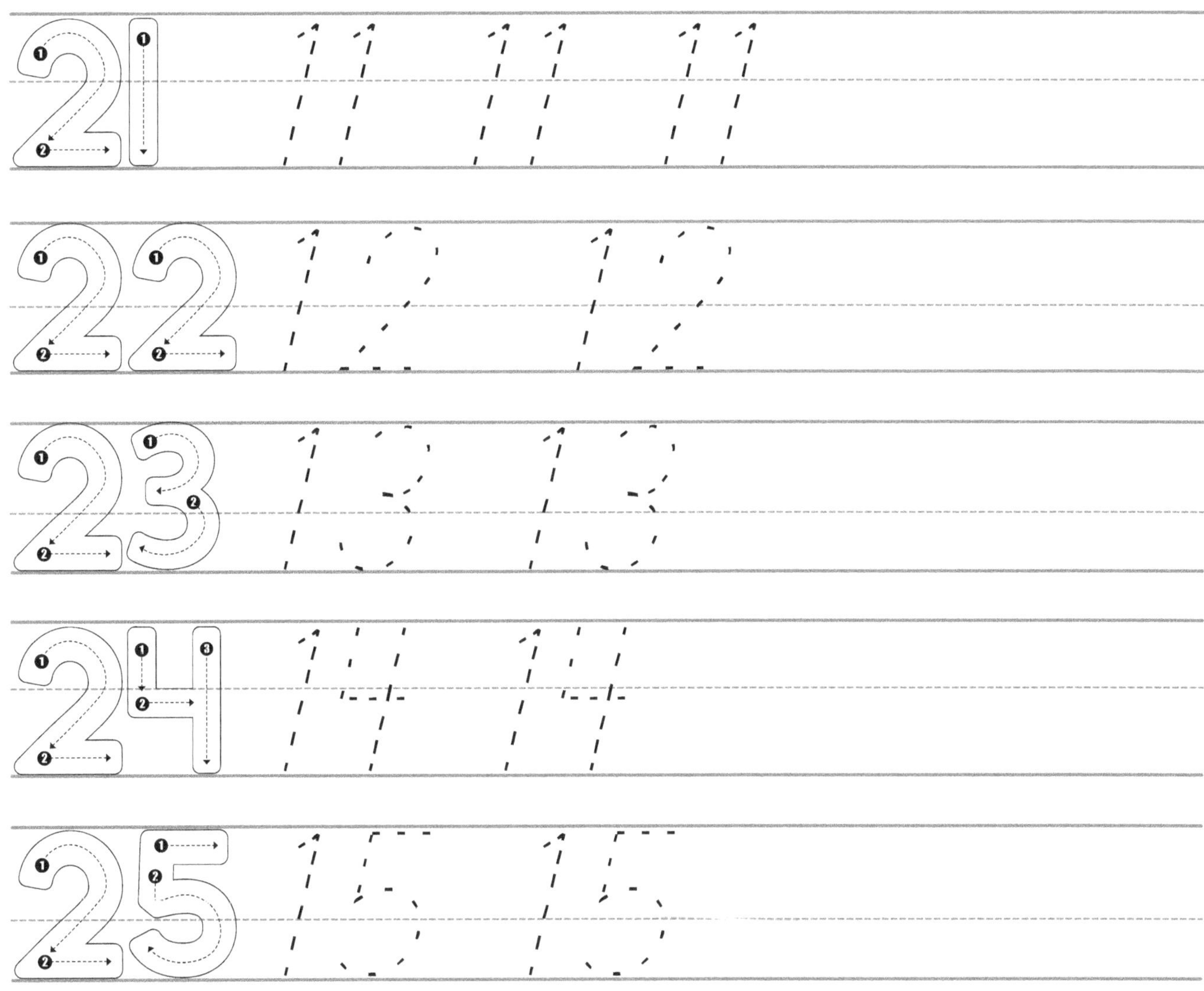

21 11 11 11
22 12 12 12
23 13 13 13
24 14 14 14
25 15 15 15

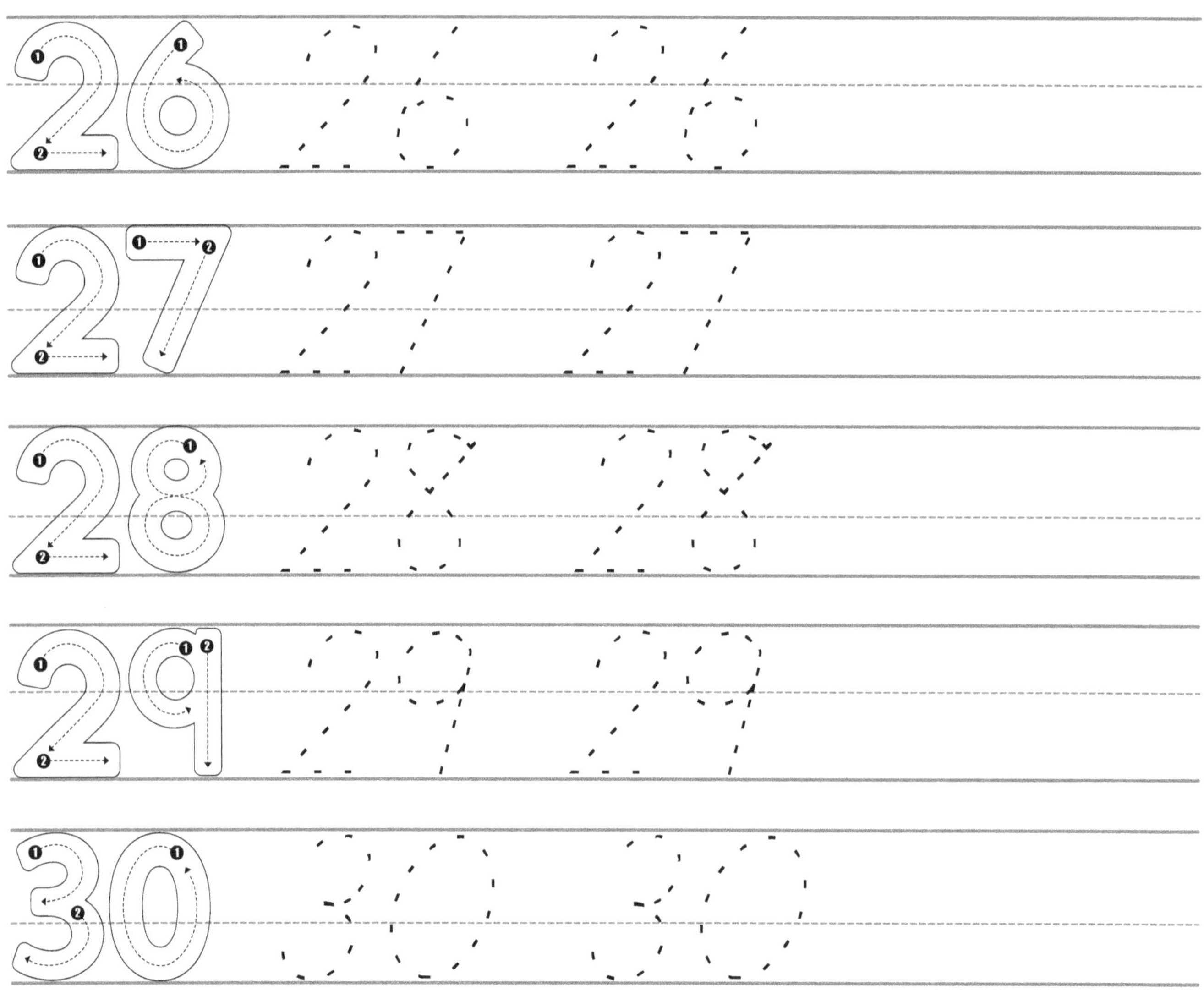

Name:

Date:

Trace the numbers and then practice writing them on your own in the remaining space!

Name:

Date:

Trace the numbers and then practice writing them on your own in the remaining space!

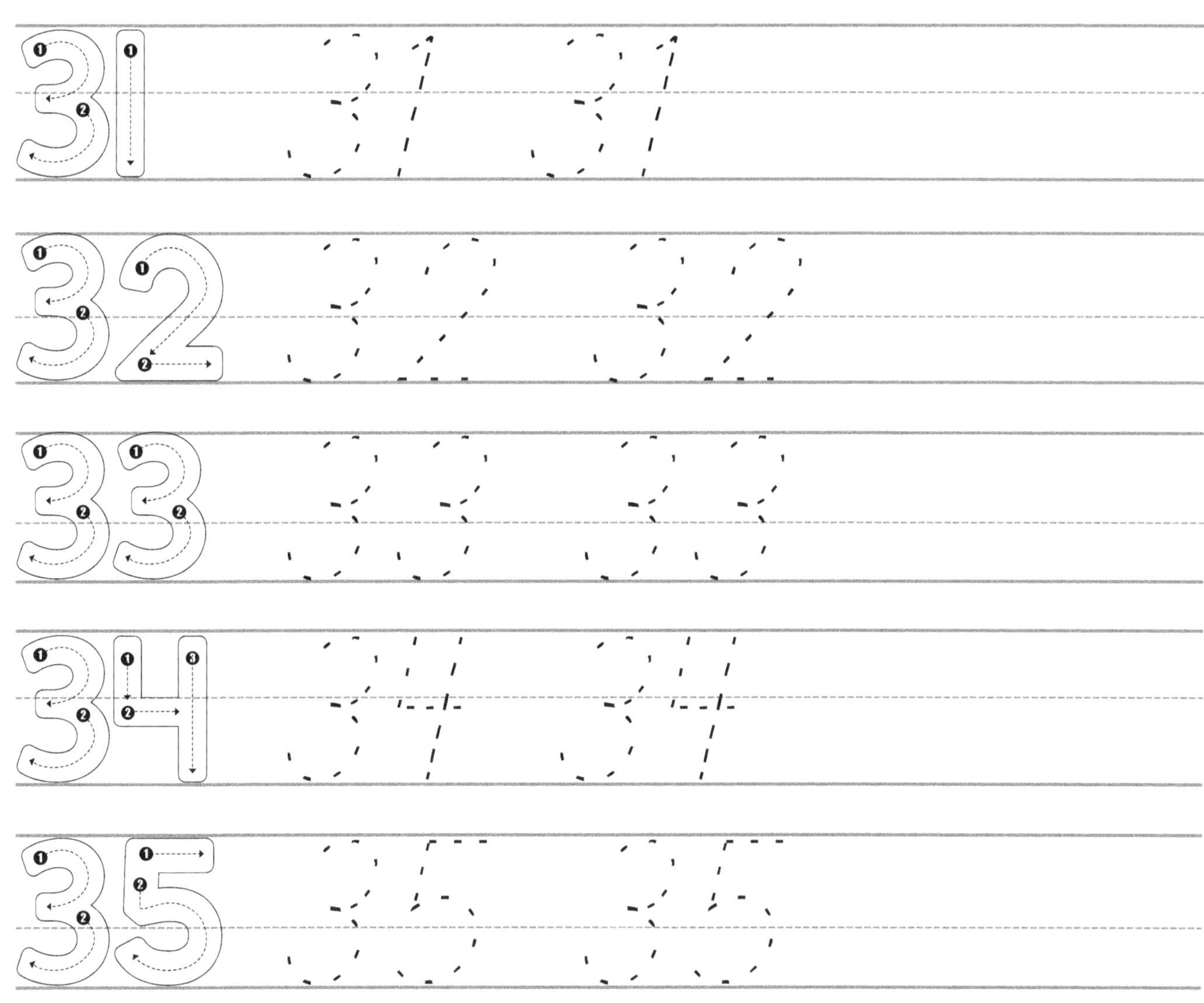

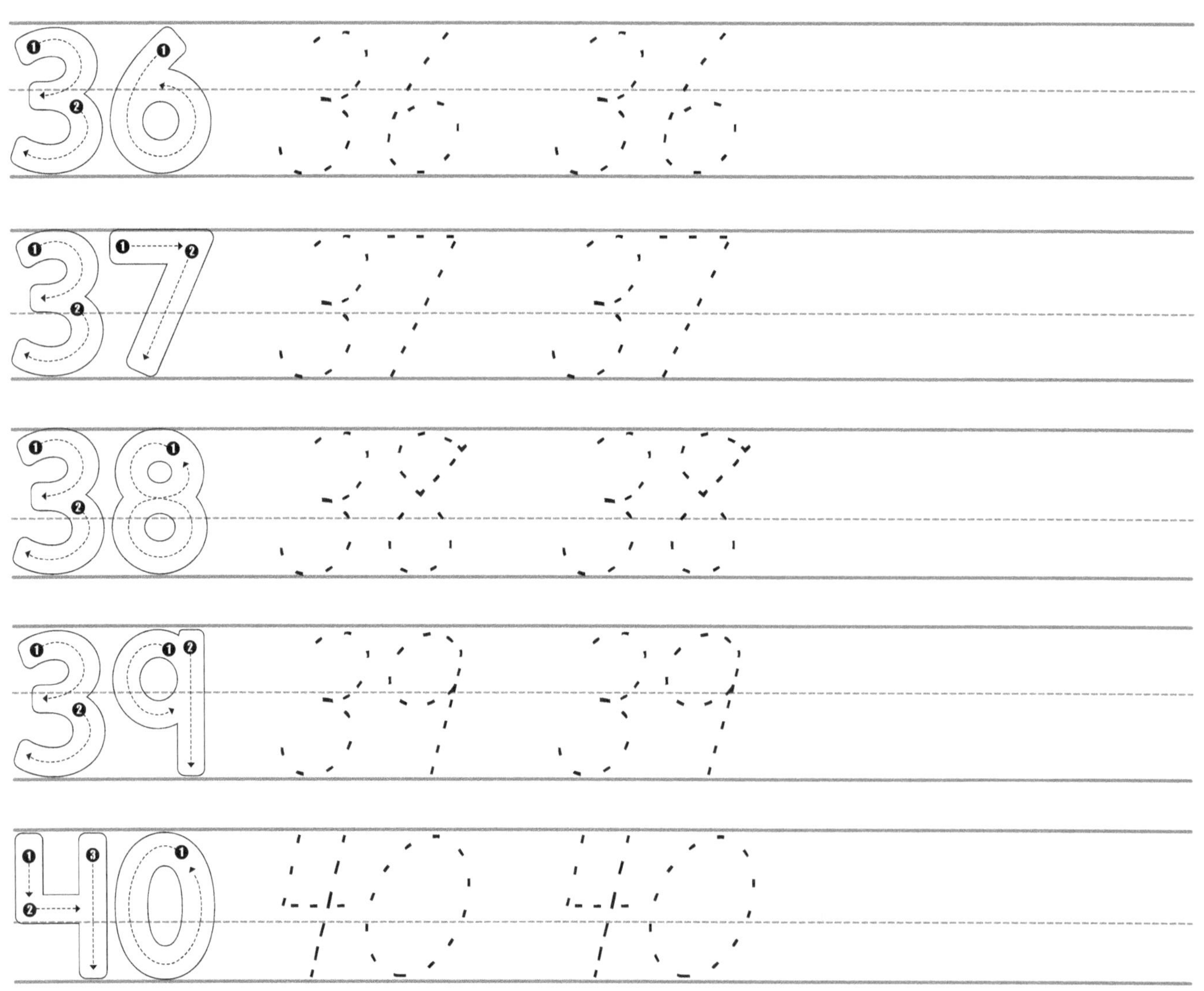

Name: _______________

Date: _______________

Trace the numbers and then practice writing them on your own in the remaining space!

Name:

Date:

Trace the numbers and then practice writing them on your own in the remaining space!

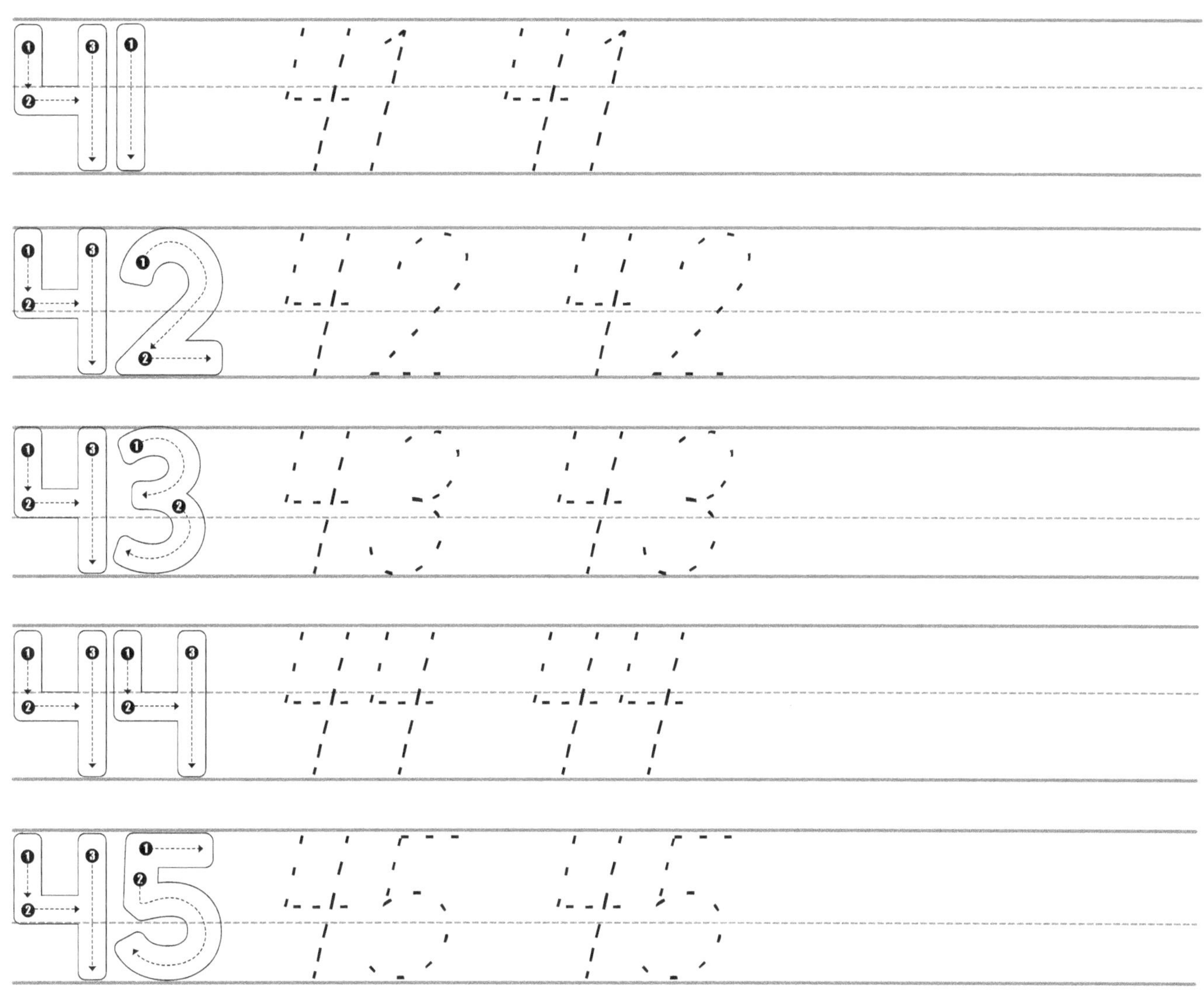

Name:

Date:

Trace the numbers and then practice writing them on your own in the remaining space!

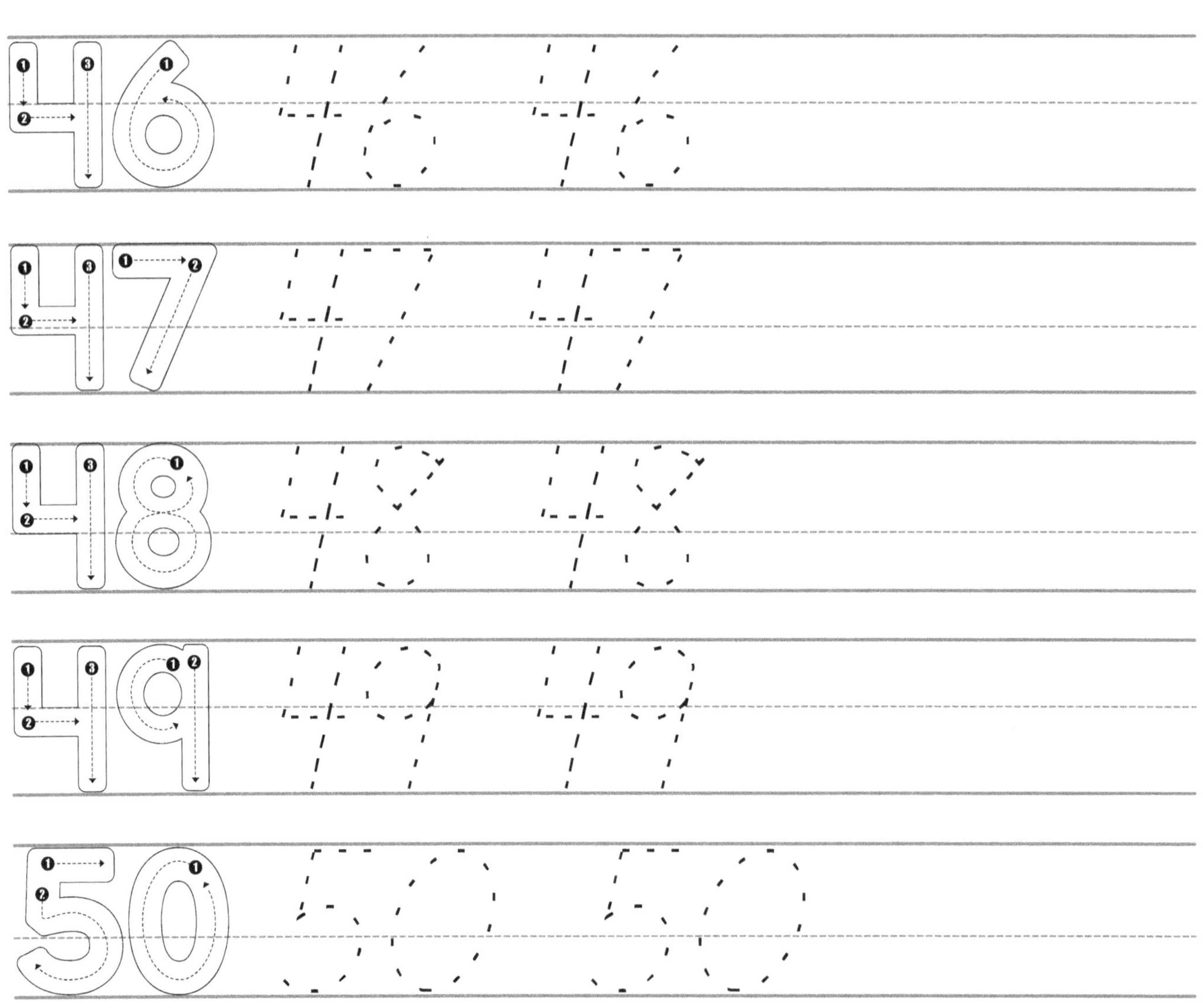

Name:

Date:

Trace the numbers and then practice writing them on your own in the remaining space!

51 51 51

52 52 52

53 53 53

54 54 54

55 55 55

Name:

Date:

Trace the numbers and then practice writing them on your own in the remaining space!

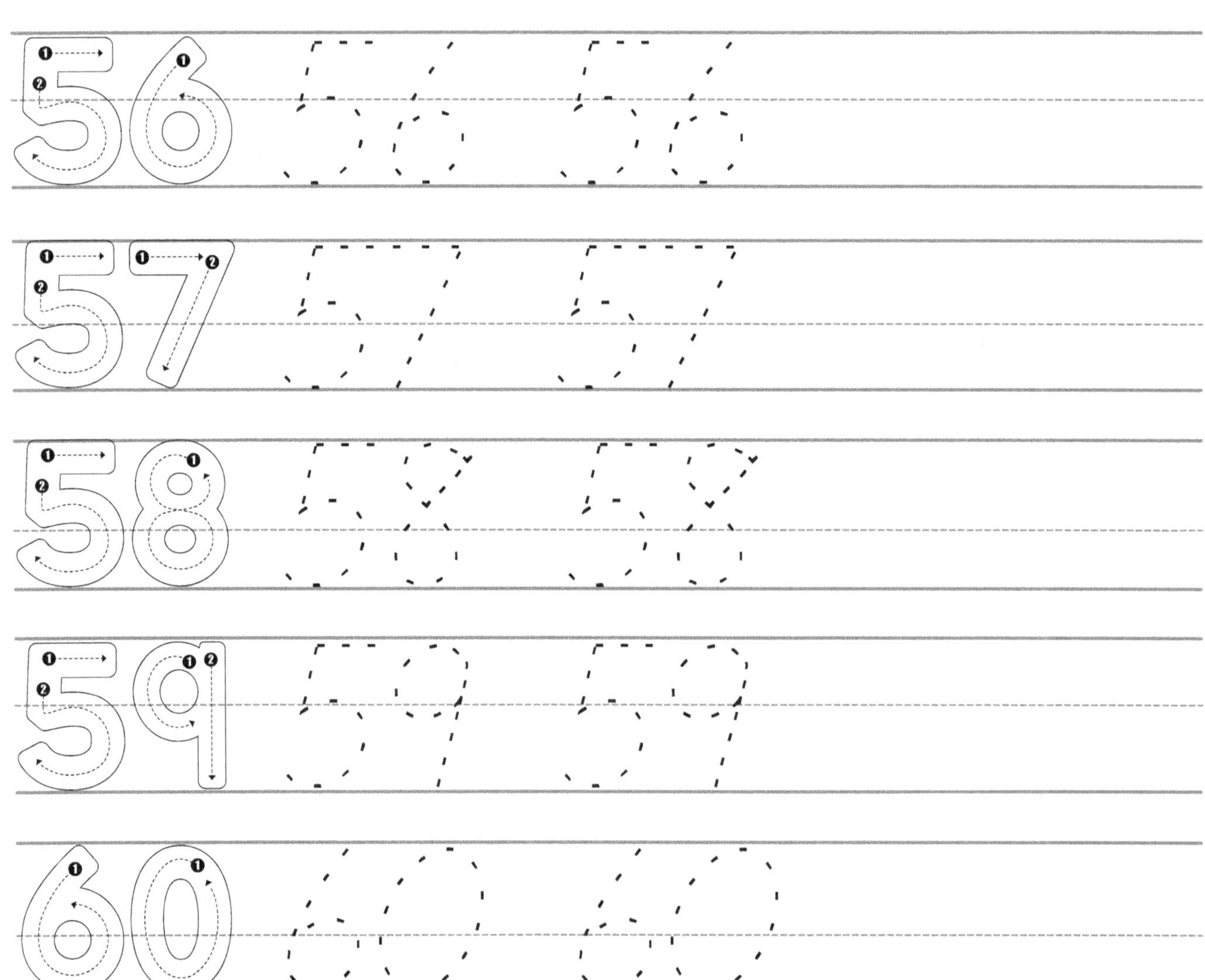

Name:

Date:

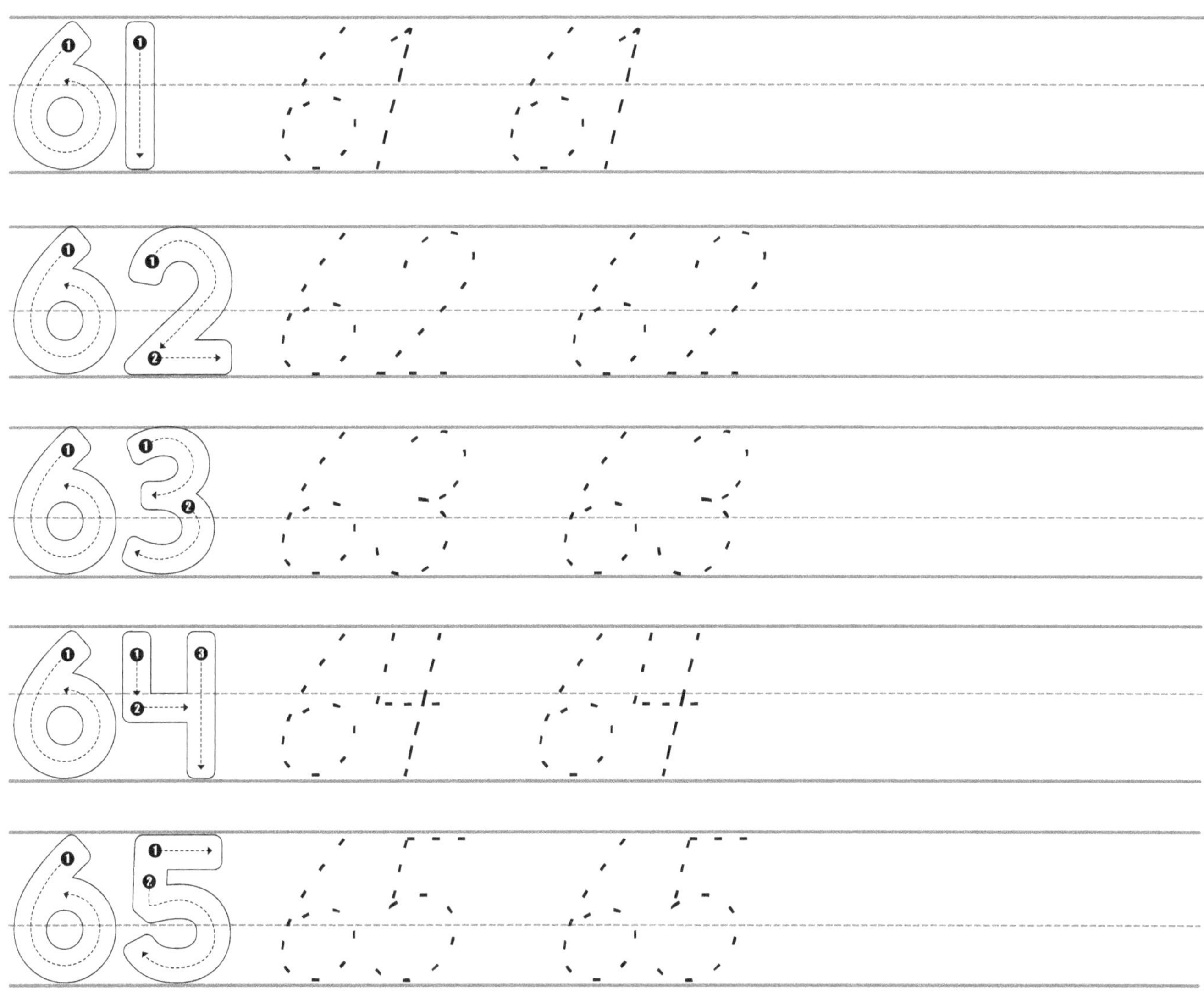

Trace the numbers and then
practice writing them on your own
in the remaining space!

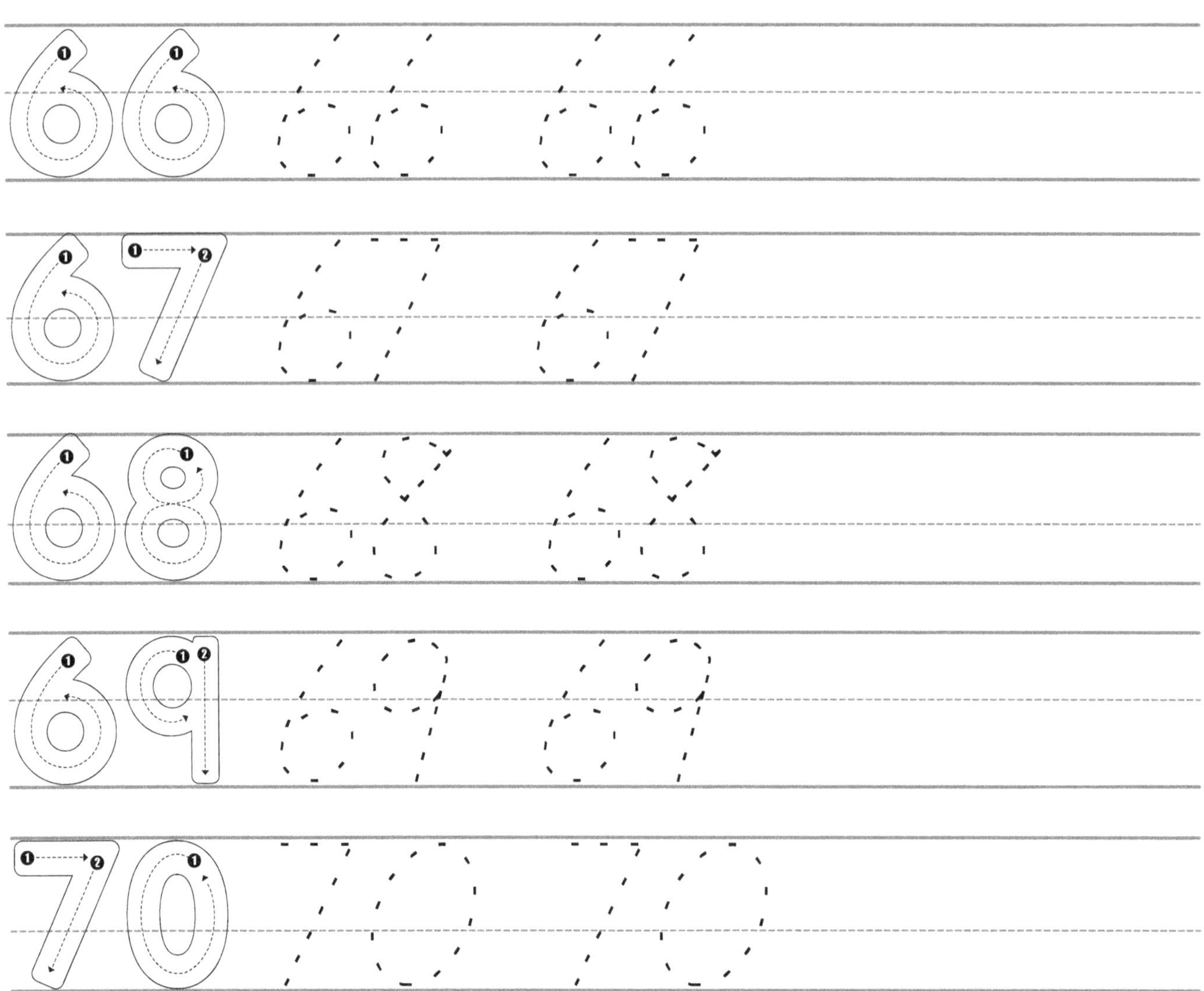

Name:

Date:

Trace the numbers and then practice writing them on your own in the remaining space!

66
67
68
69
70

Trace the numbers and then practice writing them on your own in the remaining space!

71 71 71

72 72 72

73 73 73

74 74 74

75 75 75

Trace the numbers and then practice writing them on your own in the remaining space!

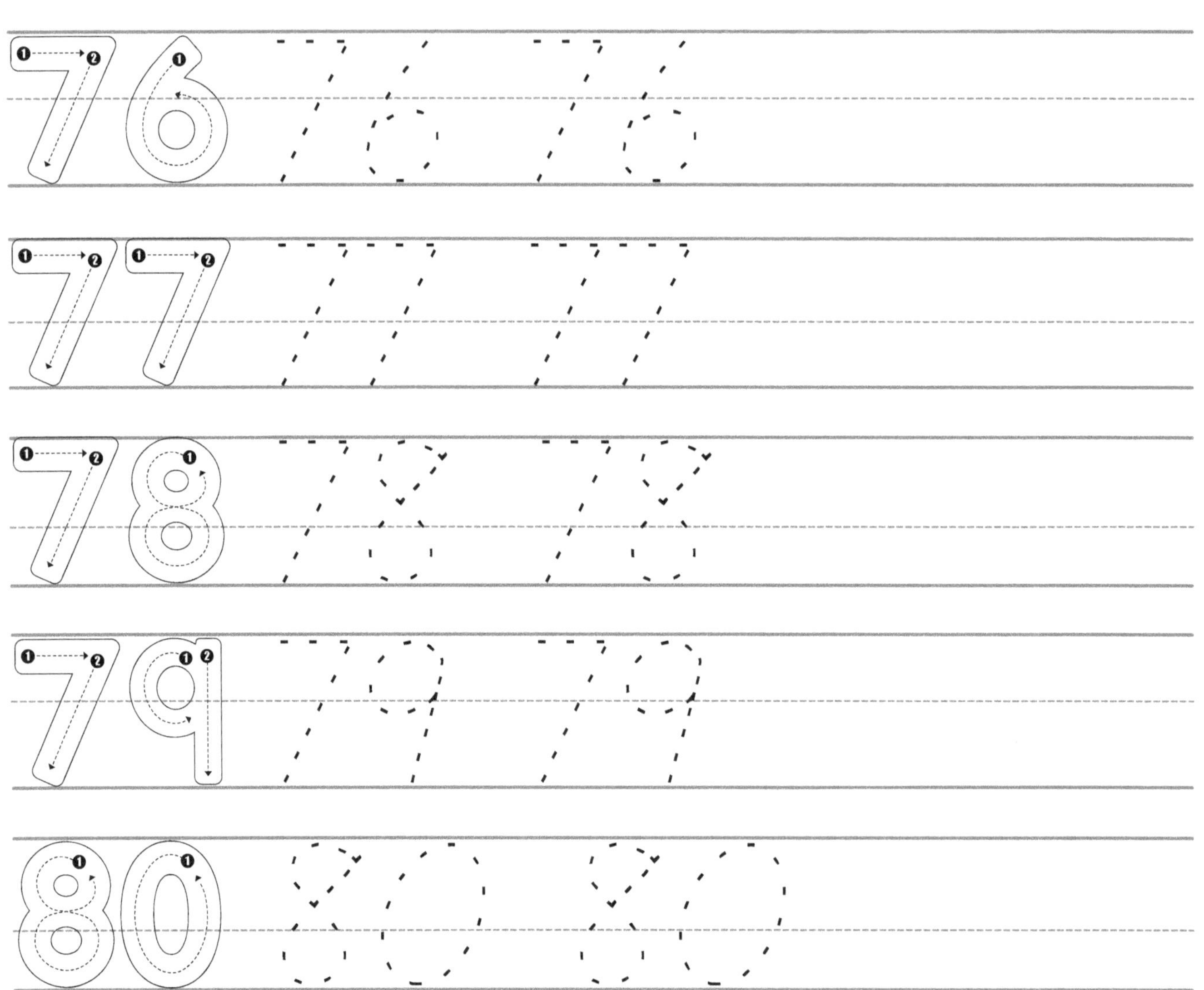

Name:

Date:

Trace the numbers and then
practice writing them on your own
in the remaining space!

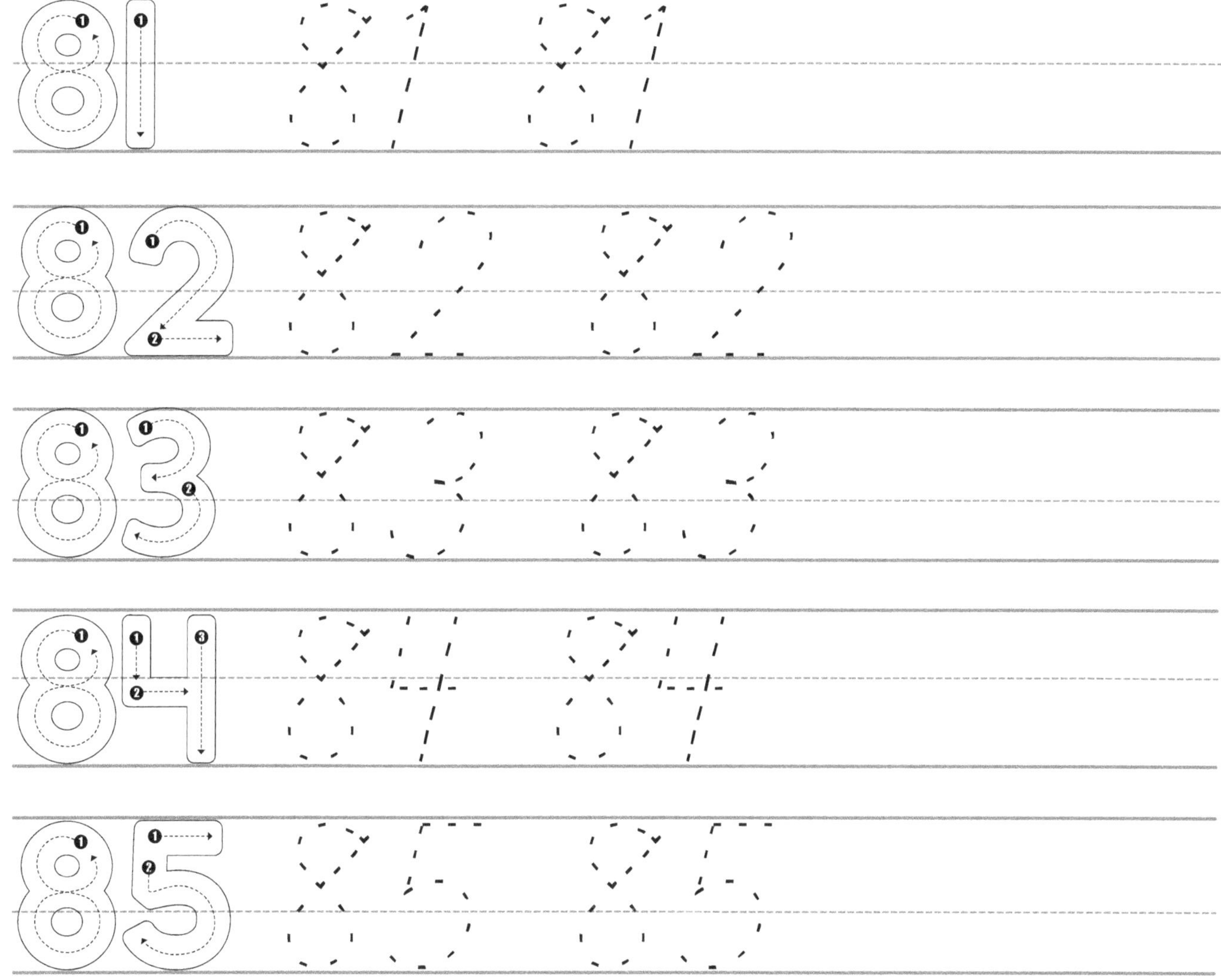

Name:

Date:

Trace the numbers and then
practice writing them on your own
in the remaining space!

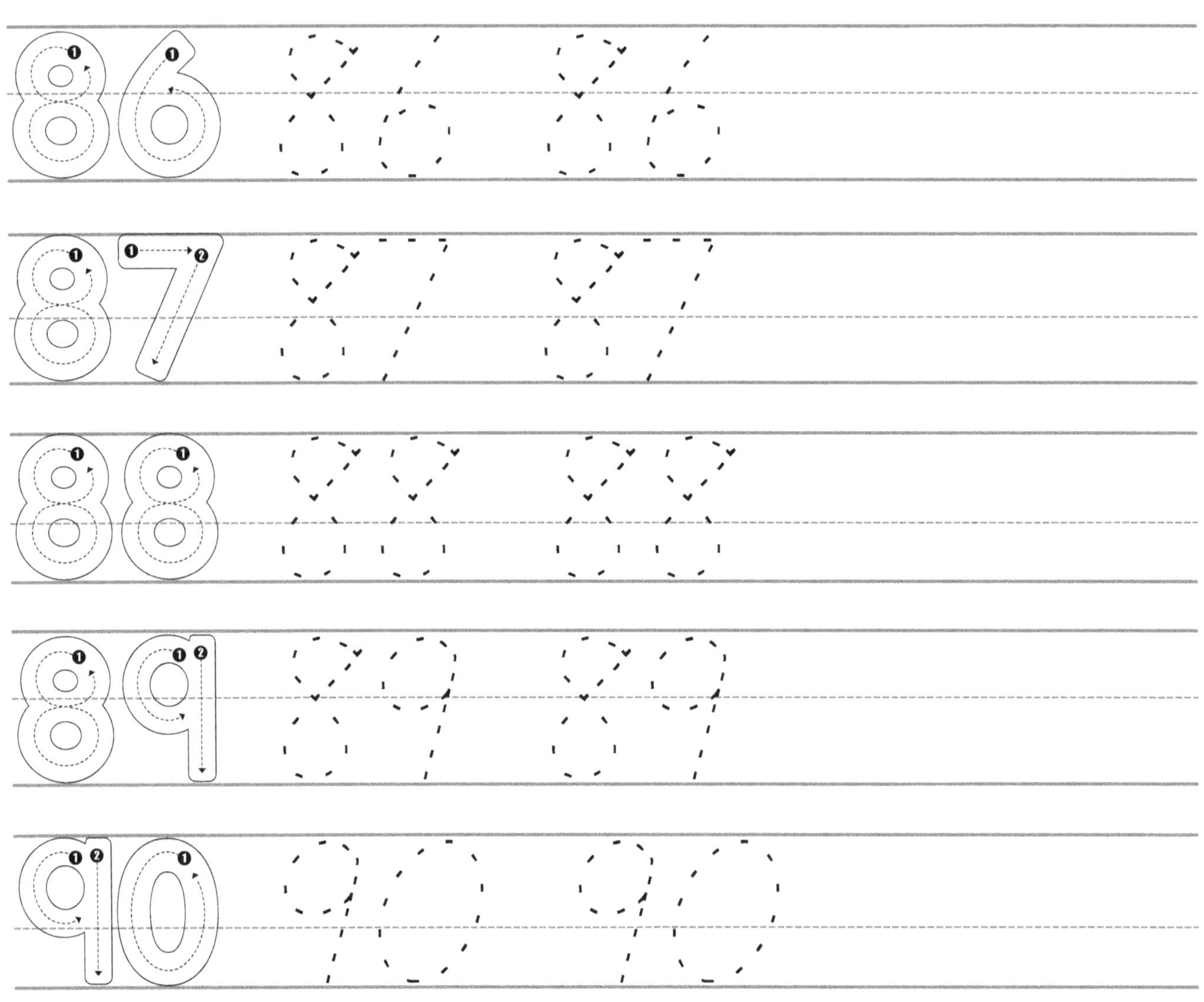

86 86 86
87 87 87
88 88 88
89 89 89
90 90 90

Trace the numbers and then practice writing them on your own in the remaining space!

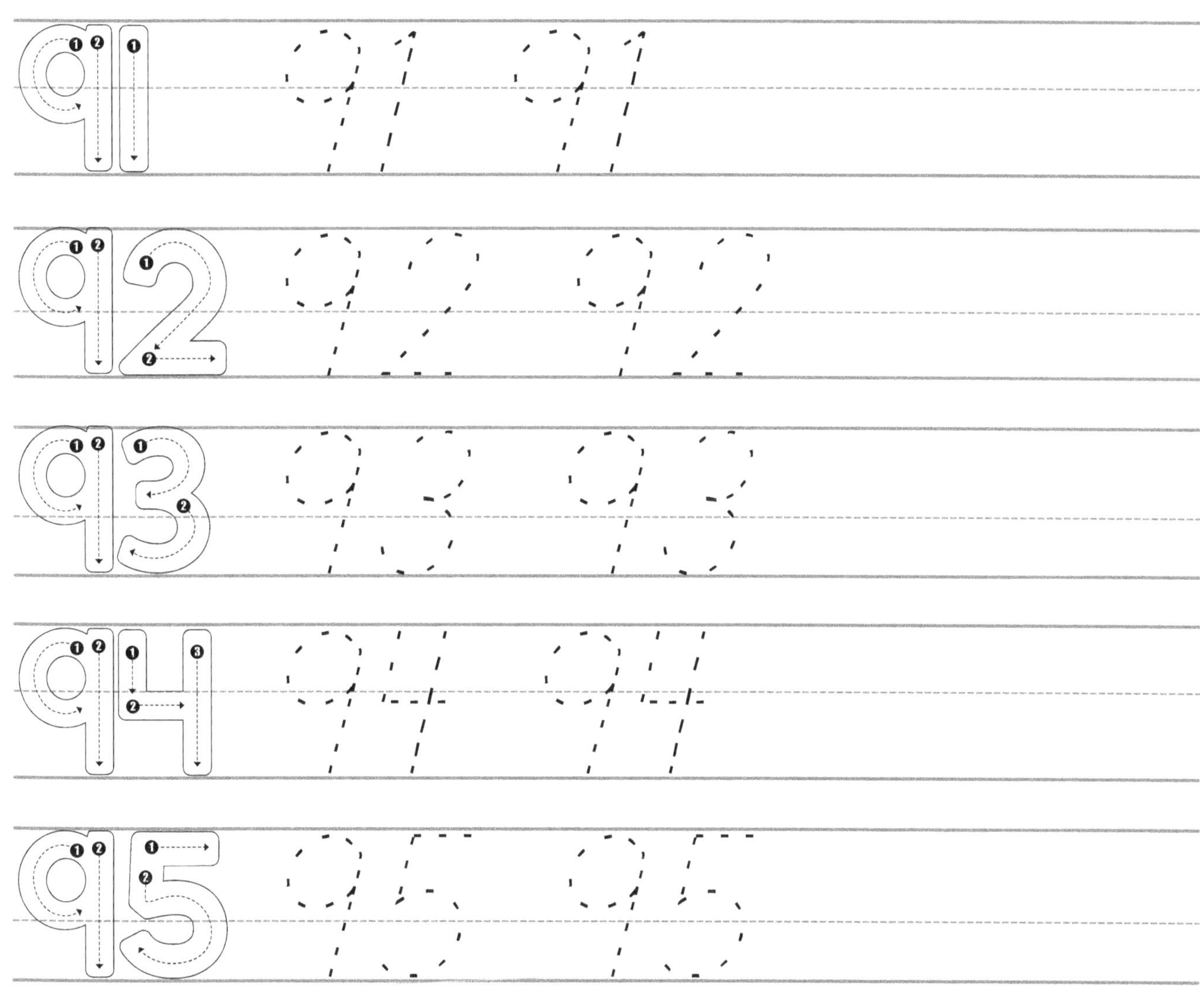

Name: ______________________

Date: ______________________

Trace the numbers and then practice writing them on your own in the remaining space!

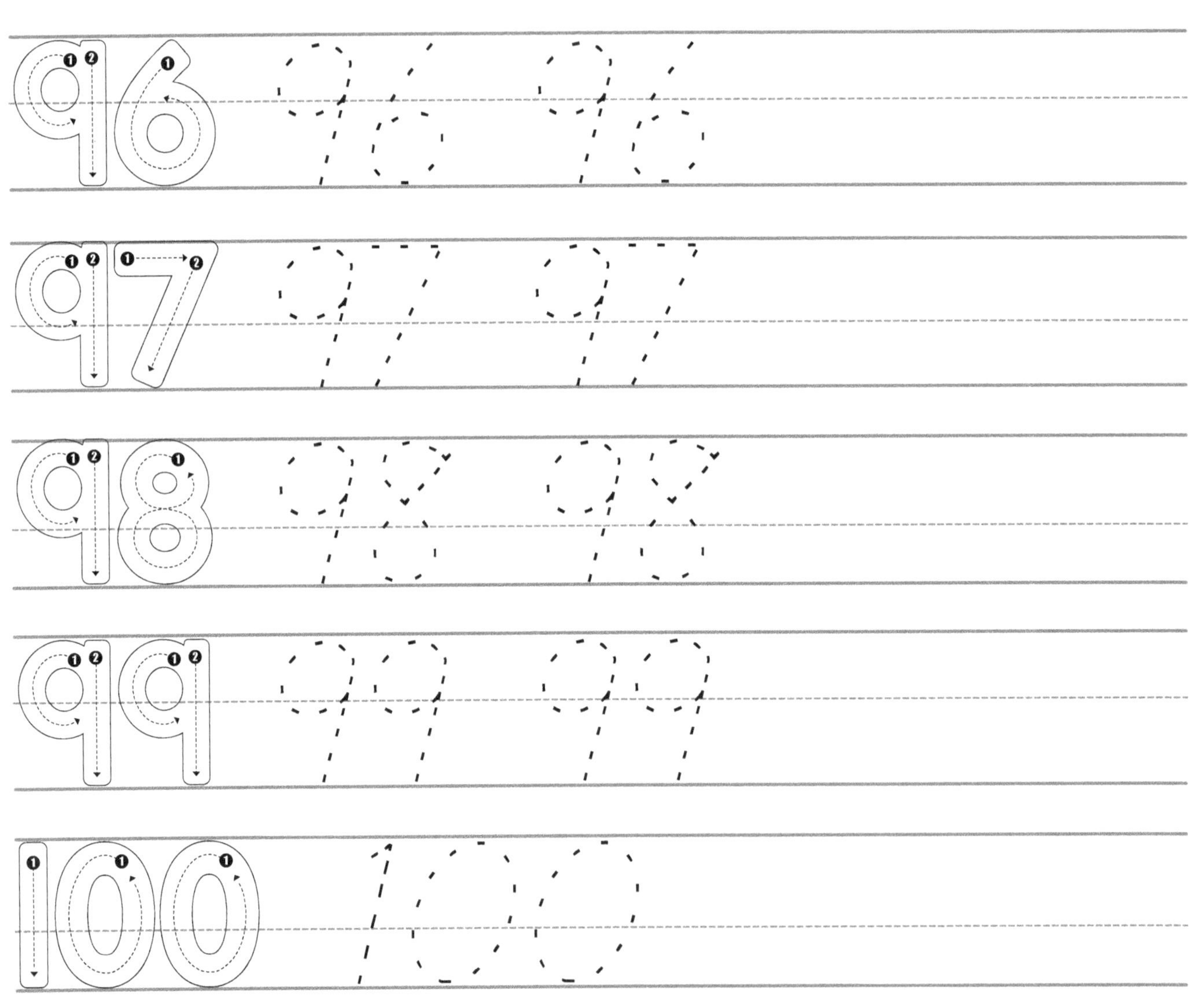

Congratulation on completing this workbook!

Don't forget to claim one of our free, ready-to-print certificates and reward your child's effort in completing our workbook. Access the link below or scan the QR code to get your free bonus!

Fonts by Artsy Pantsy

https://mailchi.mp/12abf0326fc4/certificate-of-completion